Employee Expectations
"Supervisor's Handbook"

By

JOHN T. NICHOLSON

EMPLOYEE EXPECTATIONS

Published by

Nicholson &
Nicholson Publishing
United States of America
U.S.A.

EMPLOYEE EXPECTATIONS
"Supervisor's Handbook"

ISBN-13: 978-1530384884
ISBN-10: 1530384885

First edition.

Dedication

To supervisors everywhere who strive each day to work better with and through the employees under their direction and care.

EMPLOYEE EXPECTATIONS

Table of Contents

Introduction

No matter the person.
No matter the occupation.
No matter the position.
No matter the salary level.
No matter the work environment.
All employees have certain expectations that they require of their immediate supervisor.

This is a handbook for both new and experienced supervisors alike that addresses these expectations. It is written as a reference and as a self-directed personal guide to be used as a roadmap for supervisors to better equip themselves in their role of directing others.

The sole focus of the handbook is on the expectations that each and every employee has in terms of the conditions of their employment.

It is my contention that the role of the highly successful supervisor is to simply understand and embrace these employee expectations as a cornerstone to motivate and retain good employees.

To operate a thriving business in the 21st century, whether private or public, highly successful managers and supervisors have come to understand and appreciate that good and dependable employees are without a doubt the most important resource of that business.

In fact, many successful businesses put considerable effort into supporting and retaining good employees as a foundation of their daily operations.

The leadership teams of the most profitable and elite organizations in this country put a premium on managers and supervisors who can interact with employees and get the best out of each and every individual within the organization.

In short, these successful businesses understand that employees have working conditions that they expect to be met by their immediate supervisor as terms of their employment.

For example, in the sports world it is easy to see the premium that teams put on good players and coaches. Top dollars are paid for players deemed essential for success to enable the team to reach the Super Bowl or the World Series; and likewise is true for good coaches.

At the end of this last NFL season something like five (5) NFL coaches lost their jobs because the team owners felt that a change was needed in how their team was coached in terms of getting the most of their players.

The firings were very public, came very swiftly at the end of the season, and openly serve as evidence of this fact.

Thus, smart business owners, whether in professional sports or in the manufacturing of carpet, understand the value of having management teams that recognize the importance of good employees and know just how to get the best out of each and every one of those employees.

So, for all you supervisors, and new supervisor want-to-be's, I want to share a little secret with you that can greatly improve your chances of being a highly successful supervisor in terms of supporting and guiding those employees under your direction and care.

The good news is that this secret is not rocket science and is staring you in the face as a supervisor on a daily basis. It's simply your job to recognize the various aspects of this secret and then take positive action on it.

EMPLOYEE EXPECTATIONS

So what are we talking about?

The little secret with very powerful connotations in the workplace in terms of supporting and getting the best out of each and every employee is simply this:

All employees have certain expectations of those that supervise them!!!!

So now that I have told you the secret, all you have to do as a supervisor is to work to meet each and every one of these recognized expectations in your normal course of doing your job.

And to do so not just once a month or twice a year, but each and every day you report to work.

Simple, right?

Well the answer is both "yes" and "no."

And that is what this book is all about. I want to share with you the six basic principles of meeting employee expectations; and in the process help you to create a more productive and harmonious workforce.

It is my belief that in the process of examining these employee expectations, you will be able to understand and adopt these six simple principles as outlined in the chapters to come.

And even though others may want to state that there are additional employee expectations that should be included in the discussion, I believe, and based on my direct experience supervising others under a variety of circumstances and businesses, that an understanding of these **six** basic employee expectations is the **KEY;** and encompasses everything that you will need to know.

Directly stated, adoption of these identified principles will enable you as a supervisor of employees to improve interactions with those you supervise in order to successfully meet employee expectations.

It will also make you a more productive supervisor in other ways as well, and I predict you will find far more enjoyment in supervising others just by following the principles outlined in this writing.

So as I begin this discussion let me be crystal clear and repeat the following statement:

All employees have certain expectations of those that supervise them!!!!

Even you as a supervisor yourself, and an employee of your organization, have these same expectations of your immediate "boss."

You may have never really taken the time to examine and reflect on these expectations, but that does not make them less real.

This concept that all employees have certain expectations of their supervisor is not imaginary but is very real and quite important for employees to be successful and to be able to reach their full potential. The vocation is irrelevant.

Meeting employee expectations is thus not only important, it is... VITAL... to the continued success of any organization or workplace.

EMPLOYEE EXPECTATIONS

And yet even though there are positive examples to draw from, the overwhelming number of employers from around the world, in companies large and small, private or governmental, for profit or nonprofit; etc spend very little time, if any, to train new and experienced supervisors on the principles of meeting employee expectations.

Sad, totally sad.

Employers spend countless dollars on equipment and other material resources essential to carry out the mission or goals of their organizations. And yet they spent little time or money to address and invest in the basic satisfaction needs of their most important resource for success…their employees.

How supervisors relate to their employees on a daily basis is a strong predictor of how successful an organization really is in terms of the bottom line. Knowing what makes employees tick is important. Happy employees are productive employees.

Such missed opportunities result in less productivity for the organization and less satisfaction for employees and the supervisor alike; something that highly successful businesses try to avoid.

It has been my experience, working in both the private and government sectors, that employers generally do understand that training for supervisors is important to the success of their respective organizations. But such training for new and experienced supervisors usually gets lost in the hustle and bustle of completing the *business* of the company, firm or agency.

The situation reminds me of college and college professors. Universities believe that once an individual obtains a PhD in a subject matter area, that individual automatically can then teach students in a formal classroom setting.

After all, these same individuals are experts in their fields. Passing that knowledge on to others should be a piece of cake.

What is remarkable about this perception is the fact that it is totally ***false***.

Every individual that has ever gone to college has had at least one or two professors that were absolute horrible instructors. Having a degree and being able to teach are two totally distinct attributes.

In order to be licensed to teach in high school, all teachers must be licensed in the state in which they teach. As part of the licensure process, they are required to take and pass classes on classroom instruction. You know, "*how to teach.*"

These same individuals are even required to successfully complete "*practice teaching*" under the tutelage of another state licensed teacher for a given period of time before they can even apply for an official teaching license issued by the state.

In college, no such requirement exists to take and pass specific education classes. As a result, most professors are woefully unprepared to teach let alone interact with students.

Something similar happens in the business world. Employees that are excellent in their respective fields are promoted based on solid job performance; and with promotion often comes the added responsibilities of supervising others. But these same high performers have never been properly trained on employee supervision!!!

11

EMPLOYEE EXPECTATIONS

Let me be blunt. Everyone talks about providing training for supervisors and interactions with employees, but nobody ever does anything about it.

Sure companies/businesses may send new supervisors to some management course offered by some private sector vendor over a one or two day period of time. And perhaps during that course some discussions will take place on topics like: time and attendance, workforce planning, telework policies, prohibited personnel practices, team building, customer service, strategic thinking; etc.

Now these topics are all good for supervisors and managers to be engaged in but they don't get at the heart of how to motivate and keep good employees.

These training courses spend so precious little time addressing the most important aspect of any business...***the employees,*** and **what employees expect from their immediate supervisor in order to be successful and highly motivated employees.**

Ladies and gentlemen. It all starts and ends with how employers and their immediate supervisors address ***employee expectations***.

What is it that employees want and need in order to be successful in their jobs; and at the same time be happy and proud of the work that they do and the accomplishments they achieve?

Well, let's get right to it.

These are the six expectations that employees want and desire from their supervisor:

12

1. ***To Be Treated Equitably, Fairly and with Dignity and Respect.***

2. ***To Know What Their Job Is.***

3. ***To Know When They Are Doing a Good Job.***

4. ***To Know When They Are Doing a Poor Job.***

5. ***To Have the Training Needed.***

6. ***To Work Under Safe Conditions and Have the Necessary Equipment and Resources.***

Over the course of this book we will examine these six expectations in more detail and will provide real life case studies from my experience, both good and bad, relating to each of these six expectations.

In this way I will be able to provide you with actual work related experiences to depict the different aspects of employee expectations in a manner that may have a more direct meaning to you; and at the same time lead to a better understanding of the principals involved.

The names and organizations listed in these case studies have been changed so as not to reflect directly on any one individual, company or organization.

The intent of these case studies is only to provide points of discussion, not to promote or diminish the accomplishments or challenges faced by those directly involved in such reflections in the real business world.

Chapter 1- First Expectation

"To Be Treated Equitably, Fairly and with Dignity and Respect."

This expectation is more than just words on a piece of paper. It represents a whole culture within the organization you work for and how management interacts with the "*worker bees*."

There is little doubt that if you as a supervisor violate or disregard this expectation you can damage and possibly even totally destroy the working relationship you have with your employees. Such damage can be so severe that it may be impossible to repair.

On the flip side, if you adhere to the principles of meeting this expectation you may just fine you have a group of employees that will support you unconditionally and will give their very best to support you and your employer. It really is all up to you as the supervisor.

Let's begin by examining each component of this expectation individually to better enable you to understand the power of this first expectation.

To Be Treated Equitably

In the workplace all employees want to be treated equitably. This simply means that each employee wants to have an equal opportunity and an equal chance to be

14

successful as every other employee working for the same company or organization.

"When equal access is provided, harmony exists."

"When equal access is not consistently provided, conflict often arises."

From my experience, it is common for both management, and the workforce they supervise, to consider being treated *equitably* and *fairly* as the same thing. But they are not exactly the same principles and need to be separated out for reasons that I will outline for your consideration in a manner that I feel are important for a supervisor to understand as separate conditions.

It is also important to note that the expectation of being *treated equitably* begins at the time of job application and extends all the way through retirement or some other type of voluntary separation from employment.

What do I mean?

Well, think back to the time you applied for the job that you now hold. You likely had some apprehension about applying for your job and whether or not you as an applicant would get an equal opportunity to be considered for employment.

It is just human nature to have such apprehensions.

Why is that?

Well the answer is this.

Access and consideration for employment by applicants is often times far from being equal. To be

15

honest, you have seen it in the modern day business world time and time again, and so have I.

That doesn't make it right and it is simply counterproductive for any employer to support not giving each job applicant equal consideration for employment based on actual experiences, education, abilities, knowledge and potential.

But having said that, and even though it is not right, in is not uncommon for some applicants not to receive equal consideration during the hiring process.

Let's take a look at our first real life case study focusing on this point from a hiring standpoint.

Case Study 1.1 Unequal Hiring Opportunities.

Steven Carter was working in Human Resources (HR) for the largest manufacturing employer in a five county area. The company made gauges of all sorts and had been highly successful in that endeavor for years and years. Although not the company's real name, let's call this business *NicholsonABYZ Industries*. (This name has a nice ring to it, don't you think?)

***NicholsonABYZ Industries* employed more people than any other business in the area and jobs working there were coveted far and wide.**

In fact, it was quite common for young men and women graduating from high school to apply directly up graduation to work at the local *NicholsonABYZ Industries* plant, all of this because wages and benefits were considered so darn good.

16

So good in fact that very few other employers in the area could match them.

Now Steven Carter was a local boy and graduated from St. Thomas High School, He was directly responsible for the hiring of nearly 100% of the labor force for the plant. And whenever Steven saw an applicant's name come across his desk who was a graduate of his former high school, Steve would raise that name to the top of the applicant list and he would then fill the next job opening with those applicants that had graduated from his old high school.

Other applicants, even if better qualified with more on-the-job work experience, were simply placed lower on the list and might not even be considered for positions with the company at all.

Through Steven Carter, *NicholsonABYZ Industries* practiced unequal hiring practices that gave a distinct and sometimes total advantage to St. Thomas High School alums.

To be fair, Steven would every now and then mix in an applicant or two who graduated from other high schools and offer them jobs, especially when there were multiple positions to be filled at the same time in order to make his hiring practices look legit; but eventually it all caught up to him. It took a while but his unequal treatment of potential new hires led to Steven's downfall.

You see hiring based solely on being an alum of St. Thomas High School meant that Steven ultimately hired some very poor employees while overlooking some really top notch candidates.

EMPLOYEE EXPECTATIONS

As a direct result and because employee personal problems kept surfacing, upper management at *NicholsonABYZ Industries* looked into why so many new hires were not working out. And that is when management discovered the factors Steven was using to make new hires.

The end result of the management review of the company's hiring practices used by Steven Carter was eye opening for Steven, and not in a positive way.

He was soon removed from his role of hiring new employees and given other duties. It was just that simple and that complex all at the same time.

As disappointing as it was to all those applicants that did not get hired based on where they went to high school, the hiring decisions made by Steven Carter were not the only negative aspects of his actions.

Most of the current employees noticed that the preponderance of new high hires came from the same small high school as Carter. This observation became a truly negative motivating factor for those same veteran employees who were not St. Thomas alums.

Remember that I eluded earlier in this case study that *NicholsonABYZ Industries* was the employer of choice in a five county area and the jobs at the company were highly coveted?

Image how you would feel as a current *NicholsonABYZ Industries* employee if a relative or friend of yours was denied an opportunity to be hired at the company you work for because they went to the wrong high school?

Would you feel that the hiring process was unequally being applied to all job applicants and that your friends or family members trying to hire on were being cheated out of the chance to work for the company?

Would you as a current employee be motivated to put in extra efforts at the company as a direct result of this unequal treatment?

Or would you just be thankful that you had a job and let things just slide?

Let's take a look at the business of being treated equitably in another case study addressing unequal work assignments.

Case Study 1.2 Unequal Work Assignments

Jesse Baudette worked as an engineer for the large *Blackwell & Bennett ERT* engineering firm located on the east coast. *Blackwell & Bennett ERT,* among other things, provided onsite engineering assistance to rural clients.

Jesse was a valuable employee for the firm. He was competent at his job. He worked well with people and he could think on his feet. Jesse always completed projects on time and under budget.

Now as it happens in all work environments, some assignments are more "plum" than others. Some clients are easier to work with; and some work locations are more desirable to work at.

In Jesse's case and since his supervisor never read this book, Jesse was always assigned the most difficult jobs with clients that were hard to work with; or the location of the job was the pits.

In fact, in most cases it was a combination of both of these factors added together that made these assignment challenging.

Why was Jesses usually assigned to the tough and less desirable assignments?

Well, many of Jesse's peers were slackers and would do whatever they could not to have to put in any more effort than absolutely necessary. And if there was a really tough assignment, they would drag their heels or put in a mediocre effort.

Often times, if these same employees had to deal with a difficult client they would throw up their hands and simply give up; or they would say something to the client that caused considerable friction and then subsequently the completion of these same jobs would fall back into the lap of the immediate supervisor.

As a direct result of the kind of work performance of solid employees like Jesse, compared to the slackers, management decided to then make decisions on work assignments based on getting the desired customer response with the least amount of hassle.

In this case, the supervisor in charge took the easy way out for himself and found it was just simpler not to not deal with his challenging and lazy subordinates. He thus just let Jesse handle all of the tough assignments.

And since Jesse never complained and just did his job in spite of the fact that he was being taken advantage of by both his supervisor and his

coworkers, his immediate supervisor kept overburdening poor Jesse.

Unfortunately this case study, or something similar, happens every day in the workforce across this country. The good employee is commonly asked to do more than his/her fair share in order to cover up for employees who are less motivated, less competent or are simply lazy.

Not giving employees equal access to work assignments, those assignments that are difficult as well as those that are plum, is not treating employees equally and is wrong. It has been my observation that only weak minded supervisors would do such a thing.

But let me be clear.

I have seen countless supervisors, at all levels within an organization, be guilty of this very thing. Their excuse is simply this. They say there are deadlines to meet and they don't have time to deal with their lesser performing employees. They must get the work done and the sooner the better; and so they assign the work to those that will not let them down. Regardless if the workload is equitable or not.

Trust me when I say this. Employees like Jesse will eventually get fed up. Not 50% of the time. Not 75% of the time, but 100% of the time.

Not treating employees equal in terms of job assignments is like *kissing an empty light socket.* The supervisor is heading for the shock of his/her supervisor life. It is not a matter of "if", but "when" that jolt will come.

In Jesse's case, he eventually decided to leave *Blackwell & Bennett ERT* and seek employment elsewhere. After some time, he simply became too

21

frustrated in how his talents were being used and he simply quit. His former employer lost a truly valuable professional engineer and employee.

That loss was preventable and was mostly due to inequality in work assignments.

Jesse liked _Blackwell & Bennett ERT_ but he could no longer digest having to do most of the work while others completed less taxing work for the same salary and benefits.

Another area where I have witnessed negative employee response to unequal access to work assignments centers on short or long term temporary assignments to very desirable locations.

If a supervisor wants to cause immediate disharmony with those he/she supervises, always give the best travel assignments to the same people. Nothing gets employees riled up more than unequal travel access to highly sought after work assignments at other locations.

Getting to go to warm locations for a couple of weeks on assignment in the middle of winter for a person headquartered in Minnesota is a cherished assignment. From my experience, few Minnesotans would turn down a short term assignment in California in January!!! Almost all employees would gladly sign up to do so. Catch my drift?

Let's take a look at the next case study where we examine unequal employee recognition.

Case Study 1.3 Unequal Employee Recognition

Dennis Dingeldorf and Martha Murcer both worked as two of the top people in the leadership of their organization, *ABCX Inc*. Dennis Dingeldorf managed the accounting section and Martha Murcer managed the contracting session. Both sections were housed on the same floor, in the same building in a large city in the Midwest.

ABCX Inc understood that their most valuable asset were their employees. As part of that understanding, *ABCX Inc* had established a formal employee recognition policy. In addition, the company also had set aside a certain dollar amount for employee performance awards in terms of cash and other nonmonetary awards in the company's annual budget.

When it came to the end of the year and time to submit formal employee recognition recommendations to the company HR section for consideration, Dennis and Martha both submitted their recommendations in a timely fashion. But submitting their listing and documentation for employee recognition on time was the only similarity between the actions of the two managers.

Martha was a hard nose no nonsense type of supervisor. In her mind, employee recognition to include cash awards should only be considered in very unusual circumstances where an employee went way above what was required of them for their current position. After all, getting a salary check was reward enough for employee contributions to the organization.

And as a direct result of Martha's mindset, her recommendations for formal employee recognition each year were always very few in number.

Dennis on the other hand was newer to his position and he had a different philosophy. Each year he rated every single employee under his supervision as "outstanding" and recommended the highest cash awards available for their contributions. Every single employee received annual high value cash awards under Dennis as their supervisor.

In this case study, it is obvious that employee/management conflict in terms of unequal administration of the company recognition program was inevitable.

One day this situation blew up inside the company big time as those working for Martha complained that they too should all receive cash awards for their performance as well. They just needed to work for Dennis.

It was not their fault that they had the misfortune to work for a supervisor that did not appreciate all the hard work they did for the company.

All businesses have to wrestle with this issue from time to time. Some supervisors are easy evaluators of performance, and some supervisors are far too critical of employee performance. How the company leadership sorts this out is important to for employee morale and loyalty.

My observation is that "_all_" employees desire an opportunity to be rewarded for good job performance.

My observation is also that such recognition needs to be administered equitably to all employees regardless of who supervises them. Every employee is valuable to the success of the company and they expect an equal chance to receive monetary and other forms of recognition available for a job well done.

Plain and simple, but often times screwed up.

Let's take a look at another case study that again addresses the point of being treated equitably but from a whole different perspective that unfortunately happens much too frequently in the workplace.

Case Study 1.4 Human Resource Actions

Terry Smithly had worked for the *Latham-DEF Agency* as a technician for nearly 20 years. Terry was a dependable and competent employee that was well respected for his knowledge, skills and abilities in terms of how he carried out his job.

After 20 years, it was time for Terry to receive a grade increase and that increase had been approved by his supervisor and approved by the agency leadership. With the grade increase came more responsibility, an increase in salary and a highly deserved promotion.

The only thing holding the promotion back was the formal processing of the paperwork in the Human Resources (HR) section. It was just a matter of time and completion of the required personnel actions.

EMPLOYEE EXPECTATIONS

After a couple of months had passed and still no official paperwork coming out of Human Resources, Terry became worried that perhaps his promotion had been denied. Promotions for other employees in the agency had been processed but not his. And so he asked his immediate supervisor about the status of his promotion.

The supervisor did not have an answer and went to check with Human Resources. That's when the supervisor learned that the paperwork somehow got misplaced and Human Resources then claimed that they had never received it. Terry's supervisor was told to resubmit the paperwork and it would go on the pile with the other personnel actions and would eventually get addressed.

Who lost the paperwork for Terry's promotion *at* the *Latham-DEF* Agency is not the point of this case study. The point of this case study is that Terry's expectations were not met.

His timely promotion was held up in the bureaucracy of management to no fault of his own. Terry's paperwork had likely been lost and as a direct result his promotion had not taken place in the timeframe expected.

Did Terry have equal access to Human Resources in order to process important paperwork directly related to his career with the *Latham-DEF Agency?*

No, he did not.

Had Terry's supervisor been proactive in following up with his recommendation to ensure that the appropriate action had been taken in a timely fashion?

No, he did not.

Did that lack of equal access and attention to the promotion request have a negative impact on Terry and his career?

Yes, it did.

Did the *Latham-DEF Agency* have a process in place to ensure equal and timely processing of personnel actions for the agency consistent with company policies and employee expectations?

Not very likely.

In fact in the *Latham-DEF Agency*, the lower an employee was on the totem pole of the agency, the lower the urgency for Human Resources to process paperwork for that employee. And it was not uncommon for processed paperwork to get lost for any employee who was not part of the top leadership team.

Not great attributes for a business in terms of meeting employee expectations.

These case studies are but a few examples of the importance of treating all employees equally. Highly successful supervisors will work hard, and it is not always easy, to ensure that all employees are treated equally in terms of their employment in all phases of such employment.

Whether we are talking about access to needed equipment, training, recognition or something else, all employees expect to have equal access to be able to work and compete within the parameters of the business and the opportunities provided.

EMPLOYEE EXPECTATIONS

To Be Treated Fairly

In the workplace all employees want to be treated justly. That is to be treated fairly. This simply means that each employee wants to be treated above board without undue hardship or dismay and in a manner that makes sense to a reasonable person.

Supervisors may indeed treat all employees equally but that does not mean each employee is benefiting from fair treatment.

In my experience again, treating employees equitably and fairly can be two entirely different considerations that I offer up for your reflection.

All of us as employees have witnessed unfair treatment of employees somewhere along the line.

Sometimes such treatment was intentional, and sometimes such treatment was unintentional. The important course of action for a highly successful supervisor is to strive to treat all employees fairly and on a consistent basis.

Let's take a look at the following case study focusing on the expectation of being treated fairly.

Case Study 1.5 Correction for All.

Ms. Brownfield was the CEO of a large agricultural business named AgraGoodXYZ with offices in sixty different cities located around the state. In order to carry out the services of the business, company vehicles were located at all sixty locations.

It was common in most locations that the fleet of company vehicles was stored outside adjacent to the company headquarters at each facility for easy access by a whole host of company employees.

One June during the last week of the month, gasoline was siphoned out and stolen from the tanks of two company vehicles at the Albany location something during the night. Gasoline in the other three vehicles at the site was undisturbed.

Now this wasn't the first time that gasoline was stolen from a company vehicle across the state but it was the first time such a theft had happened at the Albany location. Such occurrences were however rare and it had been several years since the last theft occurred anywhere in the state. In fact, when such thefts did occur it generally only took place in the larger metropolitan areas.

But with the latest gasoline theft, Ms. Brownfield made a decision that she had had enough of such gasoline thefts. She would put a stop to it and overreacted. She subsequently ordered all AgraGoodXYZ vehicles be equipped with locking gas caps in every single location across the state.

Now the actions of Ms. Brownfield were equitably made across the state for all vehicles even though the overwhelming number of AgraGoodXYZ locations had never experienced a gasoline theft from one of their vehicles housed on site.

Her actions were indeed equitable but were they fair?

Was it fair to require all employees at all sixty locations to take the time to go out and purchase new off-the-shelf locking gas caps for each of their vehicles;

and then be required to install and use them as a direct result of gasoline theft at one location in June?

I can tell you this much. Requiring these locking gas caps "ticked off" employees much more than Ms. Brownfield could have imagined.

For one thing, such locking gas caps are cumbersome to use and fumble around with each and every time an employee went to the gas station and purchased gasoline. And so every time gas was purchased by a company employee, Ms. Brownfield's decision met with complaint and scorn.

Perhaps the most important point in employees' minds was the fact that everyone was being punished for something that did not directly affect them and happened at a location far away from where they lived and worked.

It was like they were all being taken to the woodshed for something they did not do.

On the flip side and in her thinking, Ms. Brownfield decided that she did not want to hear a few employees at or near the Albany location complain because they were singled out and suddenly now required to purchase and use locking gas caps, so she decided to spread her brand of problem solving to all locations across the entire state.

Now her actions were indeed equitable but they were perceived as unnecessary and unfair for statewide distribution. I get that.

I also get it that as the CEO she had every right to direct AgraGoodXYZ in whatever direction she deemed fit. And I will defend her right as the CEO to make such a decision. But this decision was not fair and was a burden for all employees to adopt statewide because of the most recent incident at one location.

In my mind she would have been better off addressing the situation at the Albany location as an isolated event and move on. Treating employees equitably and fairly are two different breed of cats.

The rest of the story is this.

Four months later there was another incidence of gasoline being stolen from two AgraGoodXYZ vehicles at a location in Saratoga. But this time the results were more costly to the company.

With the locking gas caps secured on the two company vehicles, and preventing the direct siphoning off of gasoline, the thieves crawled under these two vehicles and drilled holes in the bottom of the gas tanks to get the gas. The resultant repairs to both vehicles from this single act of vandalism were over $1200 apiece.

I bet can you guess what happened next. Without her knowledge, and certainly without her permission, employees all across the state removed the locking gas caps. And Ms. Brownfield seemed to drop the whole issue as quickly as she instituted her new policy. It many ways it was just like the policy had never been implemented in the first place.

Let's look at another example concerning the expectation of being treated fairly; this time focusing on performance awards.

Case Study 1.6 No More Employee Awards.
Tom Peterson was the new company President of *GrassrootsRT Window Suppliers*. This company was a larger window supplier for the NW United States and employed over 300 employees.

EMPLOYEE EXPECTATIONS

Now *GrassrootsRT Window Suppliers* had written policies and procedures in place for employee performance recognition. The company's award program was actually very extensive and had many different options available from informal verbal recognition all the way up to significant cash awards for outstanding annual performance. These awards were administered primarily based on customer service and quality production of their brand of windows.

When Tom took over as President, one of the first conflicts he encountered was the administration of the company performance awards program. It seemed that some employees felt the system was unfair and they never got the recognition they deserved. And these same employees were quite vocal about their unhappiness.

After some time and hearing complaints from this small number of motivated employees about the company's award program, Tom made a decision. He would simply eliminate the awards program altogether for all employees. That way everyone would be treated the same and employees would have nothing more to complain about!!!!!

And that is exactly what Tom did. Within 90 days of assuming the duties as President of GrassrootsRT Window Suppliers, Tom made it official. No longer would the company have an official employee performance recognition program. Receiving a regular salary would be recognition enough.

Were Tom's actions to dissolve the company's employee recognition program equitable?

Yes, the actions taken were equitable?

Were Tom's actions perceived as fair?

No, absolutely not.

It was an annual tradition at the company to formally recognize good employee performance in this manner for years. It was expected and was very well appreciated by the over whelming majority of employees.

Abolishing the awards program was like a sudden slap in the face for most employees. It was perceived that now nobody cared if they did a good job or not. All employees were simply lumped into a single category as being "employed."

High performing employing got the same treatment as poor performing employees.

Look, administering an employee recognition program based on good performance is a proven management action that can yield many positive benefits for both the employee and the employer.

But having said that, it doesn't mean that administering such programs doesn't come with challenges because there will be challenges in making the system fair to include equal access to all employees.

Now, I personally knew Tom Peterson at the time he made the decision and took the actions that he took as outlined in the case study as listed above.

Tom had always been a supporter of the employee awards program, at least when he was lower down on the company totem pole and was often a direct recipient of such recognition. But as the new President, Tom did not want to deal with the small number of malcontents because he had a company to run. He didn't have time for their crap.

So Tom took the easy way out and shut down the company's award program for all employees.

His decision was equitable but not fair to high performing employees that went above and beyond in their daily performance of their positions.

Let's look at a third and final example of the expectation of being treated fairly from an employee discipline perspective.

Case Study 1.7 Employee Discipline

Harry was a part time employee of a large box store. One of the benefits of working at the store was that there was always free hot food in the break room for employees to enjoy when on break. And since Harry was on a limited budget and was paying his way through college while working part-time, free food was a welcomed employee benefit.

Also working at the same store were two employees that weren't as appreciative of the free break room food. These same two employees would often make a mess of the break room when they were in it, although nobody actually seemed to catch them in the act.

It got so bad at one point in time that the store manager became frustrated with the messes and decided to end the free hot food in the break room for all employees on each and every shift.

Were the manager's actions to dissolve the company's free hot foot program in the break room equitable?

Yes, the actions taken were equitable?

Were the manager's actions perceived as fair?

No, absolutely not.

Harry lost out on an employee benefit that was important to him because of no fault of his own. His peers were the culprits that caused all of the trouble and there was nothing he could do about it.

Sure the store manager treated everyone equal by ending his practice of providing free hot food in the break room. This store manager did not have to provide free hot food to his employees; and so he had every right to end the practice. He really didn't want to end the practice but felt that his employees did not appreciate the extra benefit that he was providing.

Ending the practice was not fair to all of the other employees that were not the root of the problem. It was like everyone was being punished for the actions of just two people.

I know that we as adults all recognize that life is not always fair, and certainly that is true in the workforce. Sometimes, and for very legitimate reasons, not all employees can have the same equipment, work assignments, work schedule; and the list goes on and on.

I get that, and I am sure that you do as well. But having said that let me offer these additional thoughts on the issue of fairness in the workplace.

Being treated fairly is something that is built into our psyche and culture from very early in life.

EMPLOYEE EXPECTATIONS

How often have you heard a child in grade school complain about something that happened at school that WAS NOT FAIR?

My wife teaches young people and she often talks about her students and when something goes wrong in their world, many times the focus is on something these same students perceive as unfair.

So let me be clear, unfair treatment of employees in the work place is just as important to the employees you supervise as it is to those students my wife teaches and sees on the playground.

It is just the way it is.

To Be Treated With Dignity and Respect

It was been said that in the workplace every single employee wants to be treated with dignity and respect. From my experience, I would go further and say that "*every single employee demands and expects to be treated with dignity and respect.*"

Employees expect to be valued, trusted and treated above board and in a manner that suggests that their employment is without a doubt important to the success of the business.

The overwhelming majority of employees want to succeed in their job and want to have a sense in pride in the performance of that job. They yearn to feel appreciated for the value that they bring to the organization.

In my observation of working with countless employees under many different circumstances and places of employment, being treated with dignity and respect is without a doubt crucial to the happiness and contentment of employees.

36

If supervisors mess this one up, they will fail their employees each and every time. These same supervisors will ultimately lose control of those they supervise.

I have heard professionals in the field of psychology say that:

"If you destroy a man's dignity, he has nothing left to live for."

This sentiment is true in one's personal life as well as in the workforce and is not defined or limited to just men. Dignity is important to each and every employee regardless of sex.

All of us as employees, including you as the supervisor, want to be respected and appreciated for the good work that we do.

Conversely, nothing is more damaging to the human makeup than to be ridiculed, disrespected and have our dignity degraded.

So before we examine some case studies on this point, let me give you some strongly worded advice:

"NEVER. NEVER. INSULT THE DIGNITY AND RESPECT OF AN EMPLOYEE."

Let's begin our discussion by examining and reflecting on the following case study that took place in a high school classroom setting.

EMPLOYEE EXPECTATIONS

Case Study 1.8 Poor Class Performance

Ms. Stubbing was a new high school math instructor teaching algebra-ll to upper level high school students. She was a good teacher and knew her math very well but wasn't all that experienced in how to motivate her students on a subject that could be more difficult for some than others.

In the back of her class was a young man named Johnny that seemed to understand the subject fairly well and was doing above average during the 1st quarter of the school year, but then somehow all of that changed.

Sometime during the second quarter, Johnny had taken on a part-time job after school and on weekends and seemed to be falling somewhat behind on his daily algebra assignments.

When Ms. Stubbing called on Johnny to answer a question, sometimes Johnny was unprepared and did not know the answer. It would have helped if he had completed all of his homework assignments but he usually only completed part of his daily assignments. Johnny's only response to her questions often was the same answer, *"I don't know."*

This went on for some time, particularly when Ms. Stubbing graded homework and made note that Johnny was falling behind. And it seemed that on most occasions when she called on Johnny in class, more often than not, he did not know the answer as already stated.

Johnny's non participation in class was not intentional. He just had poor study habits in terms

38

of working part-time and completing homework assignments on time. But when Ms. Stubbing kept calling on him in class, and he did not know the answer, it was all getting quite embarrassing for him. By not knowing the answers, he was publically demonstrating to his classmates that he was not with it.

After some time the situation came to a head and when Ms. Stubbing purposely called on Johnny to answer a question, she would not even give him a chance to answer. She would answer for him and would state: *"Oh, that's right. You don't know the answer."*

Ms. Stubbing had never discussed with Johnny why he suddenly was having trouble completing his math lessons and why a good student was now not really participating in her math class in the manner that she expected.

In her frustration, she decided to belittle Johnny in her math class in front of all his peers and spoke for him and did not give him the opportunity to answer for himself. Whether he had completed his assignments or not and whether he knew the answer or not, Ms. Stubbing did not want to hear from him.

From that point forward, she rarely called on Johnny and when she did she always answered for Johnny in the manner as listed above. It all seemed to be one big game, but not in Johnny's mind.

Ms. Stubbing had insulted Johnny's dignity and that lack of teacher respect was something the young

student never expected from a professional high math school teacher.

The rest of the story is truly unfortunate and sad. Johnny eventually got his act together and figured out how to complete his homework assignments and work part-time at the same time. It was difficult at first but Johnny was a smart kid and he finally got a handle on things.

But the damage was already done in Ms. Stubbing's class. She had destroyed his dignity and the respect he had for himself in that class. And he would never recover from being belittled by his teacher. The respect had been lost and it would never be regained.

At the end of the second quarter, Johnny's grade had dropped from a grade of B plus to a grade of D minus. Johnny would usually get a B or a low A on his math exams but he never turned in a homework assignment, not once.

Even though all daily homework was to be handed in and graded, Johnny never submitted his completed homework ever. Screw it. His dignity was destroyed in his mind and he would not openly participate in the class outside of taking the required math exams.

To be fair, he would also not cause trouble in class. He would just sit there and if he was ever called upon and given a chance to answer, he always stated that he "*did not know*" even when he knew the answer, but he did not otherwise disrupt the class.

At the end of the 3rd quarter his grade was again D minus. He did pretty well on the exams because he was doing is daily homework. He just would never turn that homework into his teacher for a grade and those deductions cost him dearly.

Johnny's dignity was so insulted that he was willing to nearly fail the class instead of interacting with the professional teacher that belittled him in front of his classmates. And he felt so strongly about the situation that he was willing to be removed from the prestigious National Honor Society because of his poor performance in this single class.

The above case study is something that we can all relate to based on our collective experiences in high school. Some teachers are simply ill equipped to teach.

Now let's take a look at how supervisors can insult the dignity and respect of an employee in the following case study concerning a difference of opinion.

Case Study 1.9 Difference of Opinion

Jody was the regional manager of her company and supervised eleven different local office managers in the SW region. Jody held quarterly meetings for the local office managers to discuss business items of importance and to provide needed direction and training as applicable for the needs of the company at any given time.

At the July meeting, Jody was outlining the changes that were being proposed to the company's computer system to her managers. The changes would be major and would take considerable effort to make and coordinate as needed.

These changes were met with some resistance as most managers did not want to make the changes

and learn what amounted to as a whole new computer operating system.

One particular manager, named Larry, was visibly upset about the changes. And no matter how much Jody explained that the changes were mandatory and policy, Larry was having none of it. He kept repeating that Jody should go back and tell her bosses that the new changes were unnecessary and that this region was not going to adopt them

After about the 3rd or 4th time of these unproductive outbursts from Larry, Jody stopped the meeting and reamed Larry out in front of his peers.

The verbal tongue lashing that Jody gave Larry was brutal. So brutal that nobody else in the room said a thing. They all just sat in their chairs and watched the beratement of Larry.

When the lashing was over, Larry's face was red and he was hanging his head down. He would then not participate in the rest of the meeting.

Case Studies 1.8 and 1.9 are both examples of the negative power of destroying a man's dignity. If you take away the dignity of an employee, purposefully or unintentionally, it doesn't really matter, you will lose the respect of that employee and you may never get it back.

In the case of Johnny, the case study reflects in some detail that the relationship between him and his teacher was destroyed beyond repair.

In the case with Larry, his relationship with his supervisor Jody was also destroyed beyond repair.

Please be reminded of the advice I outlined earlier.

"NEVER. NEVER. INSULT THE DIGNITY AND RESPECT OF AN EMPLOYEE."

As the supervisor, Jody did not understand this important aspect of working with employees and what employees expect from their supervisor.

Now I get it that Larry was being disruptive and wasn't supporting the decision that management had already made concerning the computer system changes. But Jody should have handled the situation differently.

From my experience and observation, a supervisor should never discipline or correct an employee in front of a crowd. And by crowd, I mean one of more other employees.

The quickest way to insult the dignity of an employee and not treat them with the respect they deserve is to correct an employee in front of other people, period.

Always make corrections in private and outside or prying eyes and ears. Both Johnny and Larry could have survived the corrections that their teacher and supervisor gave them, if those corrections had taken place in private.

Once a man or woman looses their dignity and respect, there is nothing left. THERE IS NOTHING LEFT.

And no matter what you do as a supervisor, things will never be the same or improve. That is a fact, period.

EMPLOYEE EXPECTATIONS

Summary:

"To Be Treated Equitably, Fairly and with Dignity and Respect."

All employees have expectations of their direct supervisor. This is true whether these expectations are voiced or not. And from my experience, this first expectation is the most common for both experienced as well as inexperienced supervisors to overlook or not pay heed to in one way or another. Whether this oversight is intentional or not, it will lead to failure.

Your challenge as a highly successful supervisor is do your absolute best to try and meet this expectation each and every day that you report to work.

While it is absolutely true, and based on your interactions with those that you supervise, that some days will be easier to meet this expectation than others, you can find a way to get through each and every day successfully.

For I am here to advise you that the more that you purposefully work to meet this employee expectation, the easier addressing the expectation becomes.

The good news is that highly successful supervisors have already figured this out and the relationships that they have built with their employees are truly remarkable.

Every single employee wants an equal chance to succeed in the organization.

Every single employee wants to have a fair and just work environment.

And every single employee deserves to be treated with dignity and respect and not belittled and maligned for any reason.

I have given you nine different case studies in this section for your consideration. My challenge to you is to make a brief listing of other observations that address this first expectation in your workplace, either in a positive or negative way, to bring your mind into clear focus on the operations of your particular employer.

My guess is that you will be able to make a listing of how the expectation of "***being treated equitably, fairly and with dignity and respect***" has been or is currently being violated in your place of employment.

Do this not to bring attention to the faults of management in your workplace, but to give you a reference point in your own setting that you can use as fuel to make improvements in how you supervise others.

While it is true that you cannot change how your peers supervise their employees, you can lead by example by being the best supervisor you can be.

It all starts with the understanding of this first employee expectation and then acting accordingly.

Chapter 2- Second Expectation

"To Know What Their Job Is."

This expectation should be self explanatory and easily understood, but in the reality of the workplace just the opposite is true.

It is rather astonishing how often this employee expectation is not met.

Some think the fault lies with the supervisor.

Some think the fault lies with the employee.

But in reality when this expectation is not met, it is the failure of both the supervisor and his/her employee under their direct supervision. Understanding what is expected in terms of job performance should be the foundation of providing employee direction.

We all understand that employees are given job instructions through a variety of means. Most often job instructions are given verbally but in addition there is usually some type of formal process when employees are evaluated based on some type of written listing or description of job duties.

This in true whether an employee is a part-time shelf stocker in a large box store, or is the head of the accounting department in a large law firm.

What is also true of the overwhelming majority of these written job related duties is this. The wording is usually standardized by position and is often ambiguous and difficult to understand.

46

In fact, you as the supervisor may also have difficulty understanding the written job description and position duties of your reports.

As a result, you may have a rough time explaining what the employer actually means for some of listed items included in the job requirement narrative.

In addition, and in an effort to make these formal written job duties more specific to each employee, there might be some *fill-in-the-blanks* for the supervisor to use to quantify and qualify the work expectations for each employee.

The entire process is formal and is all nice and pretty and in truth can be very useful if done properly to outline the major duties and expectations of employees.

Of course we don't want to forget the common catchall phrase that is commonly added to these formal written job duties to ensure that all bases are covered which reads something like this:

"Performs all other duties as assigned."

While it is important to satisfy the formal employee job expectation process in whatever format required by the Human Resources (HR) section, the important point is this.

Formal written job standards are only the starting point for supervisors to use in outlining specific employee job duties and what it is employees are expected to accomplish.

Let's explore the issue of making sure that employees understand what their job is and what is

47

expected of them in the performance of their assigned duties.

Have you ever heard an employee make one of the following statements?

"That's not my job."

"I didn't know I was supposed to do that.

"That's not in my job description."

"Nobody told me."

"I'm not paid to do that."

"Don't talk to me that is above my pay grade."

The answer to the question is pretty straight forward. We have all heard employees make statements similar to these from time to time and in one way shape or another.

In fact, if we are honest with ourselves, we too have said something similar as employees.

Sometimes such statements are made in jest; and sometimes such statements are made as a matter of fact.

So then you have to ask yourself.

"How can I expect employees to do the best work they possible can if they are not sure what is expected of them?"

48

It has been my observation that when things go wrong in the work place, many times it all goes back to not knowing what was supposed to have been done in the first place. The job instructions were not clear or the employee simply didn't understand what was expected and made assumptions that were incorrect.

Let's take a look at the following case study focusing on the understanding of what the job expectations were in an office setting.

Case Study 2.1 Special Company Mailing

Sherry was an administrative assistant who was given the assignment of sending mailers to customers informing them of the company's upcoming special product sale.

The sale information was sent to all of the major customers. This mailing was complete along with special discount coupons enclosed as a way of celebrating 25 years in business. This special anniversary mailing was a way the business was using to thank those customers for their patronage throughout the years the company was in business.

Now Sherry was an efficient employee and she had successfully made mass mailings to customers before. She was good at it and in no time she completed the task and had all one hundred customer letters printed out on the special 25th anniversary letterhead as well as having the envelopes stuffed, addressed, stamped, sealed and ready to go.

EMPLOYEE EXPECTATIONS

Later that day she passed off the mailing to the postal worker that delivered the company mail to the office and that mailing then went out for distribution to the selected customers.

Just before closing time later that same day, Sherry's boss came to see her and inquired about the mailing. Her boss was holding a box of uniquely made envelopes with the company logo and 25 year anniversary marking embossed on the envelopes. These envelopes were different than the standard envelopes used by the business and were specially made for this one time mailing. That is when the boss discovered that Sherry had already mailed out the special mailing.

The problem was unfortunate but obvious in the final analysis. Sherry did not know about the envelopes and that her company had them made special for such 25 year anniversary activities and promotions. If she had known, she would have waited before sending out the mailing so that the new, unique and celebratory envelops could have been used.

This case study represents a common problem in the workplace, miscommunication about a task or an assignment. Such miscommunication represents good intentions gone awry.

Sherry's company was proud to celebrate 25 years in business and had invested in marketing efforts to express appreciation to customers for their business. And Sherry had been a successful team member of this company for over 15 years was proud to be a part of the growth of the company.

But she did not know that these special 25th anniversary marketing envelopes even existed. To make matters worse, her supervisor had not given her specific instructions to use the special envelopes and most likely just overlooked that detail.

The dropped supervisor/employee communication was so simple and yet let to results that were not in line with the 25 year marketing plans of the company.

In this case, the supervisor should have taken the time to make sure that Sherry had all the materials she needed to make this one time unique mailing to customers.

The supervisor should have taken the time to make sure that Sherry understood that the mailing included the special 25th anniversary letterhead as well as the 25th anniversary envelopes as important components of the campaign.

There are several other points concerning this case file for discussion:

1. There are many short term assignments that will not, and should not, be written specifically in the formal employee performance document that outlines the duties of the employee. That would be nonproductive and quite lengthy to say the least.

No in these instances of short term and unique assignments, the specifics of the duties of such assignments will need to be communicated verbally and in an easily understood manner from supervisor to employee.

2. When the supervisor makes an assignment and that assignment is not routine and deviates from the norm, even if only slightly as in this case study, the supervisor should ask the employee if they understand the assignment and what is expected of them.

Doing such does not take a lot of time and helps to ensure that the employee is successful and the assigned task will be completed in an acceptable manner.

Sometimes supervisors will tell me that they don't like to do what I am advising because they don't want the employee to think that they are stupid. These same supervisors don't want to insult the dignity of those under their care.

Hogwash, I say.

It would not have been difficult in this case study for the supervisor to simply show Sherry the new 25th anniversary envelopes and ask her to make sure that they are used in this special mailing; and then ask if Sherry had any questions.

There is nothing insulting about doing just that. Making assumptions that employees understand an assignment that is outside of the normal manner of doing business is risky. And those supervisors that have a habit of making such assumptions will eventually get burnt, and so will the employee.

Please be reminded of the fact that the overwhelming majority of employees under your direction are motivated to do a good job.

Most employees take great pride in not making mistakes on the job. And as a supervisor it is your job to tap into that positive motivation and do what you can to assist your employees to be successful at each and every task that they do. They can only be successful if they understand what is expected of them on each and every assignment.

3. Once a mistake is made because an employee did not understand their job or what was expected of them, the supervisor should take the time to discuss the mistake and make an effort to improve the communication(s) that led to the misinformation or lack of communication with that employee.

This is not a time to lay blame, but a time to discuss how not to make the same or similar mistakes in the future.

Let me give you another quick example of this type of misunderstanding concerning job assignments.

I volunteer at a local food bank to repackage donated food for consumption by those in my community in need.

One Saturday, the group I was working with was given the assignment of repackaging hundreds of boxes of cereal that were labeled incorrectly.

It seems that the major manufacturer of the cereal was processing a popular cereal in boxes that you would normally buy on a typical grocery store shelf, only in this case the cereal boxes in question were labeled gluten free.

The only problem was that the cereal that was actually put into these same boxes was not gluten free.

The end result was that this major cereal company couldn't sell the product because of the labeling error, and thus donated this particular batch of mislabeled cereal to the local food bank for repackaging and distribution to those in need as cereal containing gluten.

It was explained to me that a new employee was in charge of the production line on the day the cereal was boxed in the wrong containers. This new employee had no idea that there were different cereal boxes for cereal that focused on what was gluten free and what was not.

Somewhere along the line, the supervisor of this employee had made an assumption that all the aspects of cereal packaging for gluten free vs. regular cereal was apparent to the employee in charge of the production line on the day of this particular cereal run.

That was a costly assumption and quite frankly not the fault of the employee.

The following is another case study that depicts problems that can occur when an employee does not understand what is expected of them.

Case Study 2.2 Pick and Choose

Derrick and I worked for the same organization. In fact, I was Derrick's brand new and immediate supervisor. He was a veteran employee with good

jobs skills and had mastered most aspects of his job rather well.

Derrick just had one shortcoming that I considered rather major. Derrick had this habit of only doing those aspects of his job that he really wanted to do. Those that he didn't want to do, he let slide. His mode of operation was to let somebody else complete the tasks that he did not want to do.

Shortly after I started working with Derrick, it became abundantly clear that I had an employee that was not addressing his work assignments (tasks) associated with those tasks that he did not like to do.

In subsequent discussions with Derrick, it became clear to me that he understood that he had other tasks to accomplish, and even had assigned goals to meet in terms of those same tasks. His position was that his past supervisors took care of the tasks he did not want to do, while he just concentrated on those that met his fancy.

When I pointed out to Derrick that it was in the best interest of our organization and the clients we served if he in fact worked to accomplish the full range of work assignments as listed in his official job description and annual performance work plan.

I went one step further and pointed out to him that the only way he could have a successful annual performance rating was for him to do his assigned tasks in totality.

EMPLOYEE EXPECTATIONS

The man was shocked. Sure he knew he had other official responsibilities but nobody ever made him do them before me. Most people just let him slide.

This case study is far from unique. The overwhelming number of employees will have assignments that vary. And it is quite true that some assignments are easier than others or more desirable. That is just a fact of employment working for someone else that pays your salary.

In this case study, Derrick had a clear understanding of his job expectations. He just purposefully chose to ignore certain job assignments. Derrick felt that he was above all of that stuff and his understanding of what was really expected from him might not be official but it was how it was.

It took a little while on my part, and an attitude adjustment of Derrick's part, but in a short period of time we came to an understanding of what is job was and what the organization expected from him.

The specifics of how I addressed Derrick's misconceptions about what his job is not the purpose of this discussion. The purpose is to point out that sometimes, employees do not want to fully embrace the total work related responsibilities of their position. If you have yet to face this situation, you will.

As a supervisor, it is your task to ensure that such efforts to skate by important aspects of the job cannot be tolerated.

What is amazing about this case study, and the heat Derrick felt from me as his new supervisor, is that is some weird sort of way, I gained a lot of respect from

Derrick himself for holding him accountable. And I can also report that the feeling was mutual.

After we came to a mutual understanding of what was expected from him, he became a fully rounded employee and one of the most productive employees I ever supervised. He actually seemed to embrace taking directions from me and I learned to ask for his advice on matters of customer service where he had far more experience.

It all started with establishing a clear understanding of job expectations.

The following case study centers on assigning goals and reporting of accomplishments tied directly a specific position.

Case Study 2.3 No Assigned Goals.

Jerry Long was one of 12 employees that worked in the engineering section under Delwin Perry as the immediate supervisor. This organization evaluated employee progress in terms of meeting certain numerical goals on a monthly, quarterly and annual basis.

These goals were listed as ten specific items as handed down to Delwin as the section head and were part of the overall production goals of the company. Each section, including the engineering section, was expected to meet their assigned goals throughout the year as evaluated and assessed monthly, quarterly and annually as already indicated.

EMPLOYEE EXPECTATIONS

Some of the goals for Delwin's section included: number of client contacts, number of new contracts written, number of services provided; etc.

To be specific, the company leadership had assigned a specific set of applicable production goals to the engineering section and left it up to Delwin to determine how best to meet the goals.

Delwin's style of management was rather loose. And as such he did not assign specific goals to each of his employees. He figured as long as the engineering section made the section goals overall, he didn't have to assign individual goals to his employees. It would all just work out in the end.

The result was predictable. The engineering section under Delwin's leadership would sometimes meet their monthly goal but would rarely meet their quarterly and annual goals. In short the engineering section was simply one of the least productive sections of the company.

The reason for this lack of successful performance by the engineering section was certainly understandable. The employees under Delwin's supervision, including Jerry Long, did not know what was specifically required of them to meet the company goals. Sure they knew that the company had goals and that these goals were something to shoot for, but not something that each one of them was specifically responsible for.

Many organizations have some type of measuring stick to determine if the organization is meeting the goals and objectives of annual and long range strategic plans.

Often times these goals and objectives are measured systematically throughout the year so that adjustments can be made where and when just adjustments are appropriate and necessary.

In this case study, the employees under Delwin's supervision were not given individual goals to achieve. These employees did not really have a clear understanding of what was being expected of them as individuals in order to meet the performance and production expectations of the engineering section and the company as a whole.

How can an employee know what their job is if they are not told?

Part of knowing what the job is undeniably centers on knowing when the employee is successful and when they are not. Meeting individual production goals is all part of the job for employees no matter whom or where they work.

In this case study, Jerry Long had no clue as to the number of client contacts, the number of new contracts written, nor the number of services provided he was expected to achieve on a monthly, quarterly and annual basis. Jerry just did his job and that was that; at least in his own mind. It would all just work out in the end.

It should again not be overlooked that the overwhelming numbers of employees want to do a good job in all that they do. And if they know what is expected of them, what their job is, they will strive to do their best.

I can tell you that in Delwin's case, if he had assigned individual goals that were fair and equitable to Jerry Long, Jerry would have met each and every goal. Month after month. Quarter after quarter. Year after year.

Jerry just didn't know that part of his job performance was to be responsible for a certain level of progress coming out of the engineering section as an individual employee, as a member of the engineering section, and a valuable team member within the company.

Here is the rest of the story.
All of the other eleven employees in the engineering section were also quite capable of meeting assigned individual goals. They were just never challenged or held accountable specifically to do just that.

The final case study in this chapter discussed formal employee performance plans and some of the issues such plans present to both the employee as well as the supervisor.

Case Study 2.4 Formal Performance Plans.
Elizabeth supervised six employees and each year she was required to develop an annual written individual performance plan with each of her reports at the beginning of the performance year.

At the conclusion of this plan development process, she and the employee would both then sign and date the document as having reviewed and properly orchestrated the employee performance plan for the upcoming performance year.

Completing this formal process met in part the supervisor/employee performance evaluation process as required by the Human Resources section according to policy of the company.

To be sure, these individual employee performance plans were cookie cutter fill-in-the-blank type documents that were structured similarly for each employee.

Not only were these documents all similar to a large degree but they also contained language that was difficult to understand and often somewhat vague.

In fact, Elizabeth herself did not know what some of the items in these employee performance plans actually meant, and when an employee asked, she would just say: *"Don't worry about it. You will have no trouble meeting that item. I know what you are capable up."*

After each of these initial performance plan development sessions, these same six employees left their individual annual performance plan meetings with Elizabeth either frustrated, laughing or disappointed in the whole process.

These employees were always left to rely on Elizabeth to give them a fair evaluation of their performance during the year. All of this simply because they weren't ever sure what was actually expected of them because as employees they did not understand the wording used in their respective employee performance plans

The entire process seemed risky and each of her employees felt that their performance was taken out of their individual control.

EMPLOYEE EXPECTATIONS

Does this case scenario sound familiar?

Sure it does. It reflects the modern day work place in the 21st century more often than I can reflect, and it doesn't matter who the employer is.

Formal written annual employee performance plans that are developed between supervisor and employee have become so complicated that neither party has a full understanding of the content contained in these plans.

Now I understand the reasoning behind such plans. Improper termination of an employee can lead to headaches for Human Resources and may even be challenged in a court of law.

The ultimate result of such concerns has led to a collection of annual individual employees plans that are difficult to understand; but are judged as defensible in the case of a contested employee dismissal.

So who loses out?

The good employees who do their job, show up for work on time, and are the real reason the business is so successful.

Let me give you an example.

One time I took on a part time job at a big box store to get some firsthand experience of the management and employee interaction issues between supervisors and a part-time workforce that was constantly changing in an environment with a large employee turnover.

It was several weeks after I had started on the job, when my immediate supervisor called me into the break room to formally go over a single sheet of paper that outlined my job responsibilities.

Now I had never seen this particular piece of paper before but if the boss wanted to outline my formal job responsibilities on paper for me to acknowledge, I was all for it. This should be fun. I couldn't wait to see how my supervisor approached this review.

As we looked at the page together, there was a place at the bottom of the page for the supervisors to date and sign, along with a place for the employee to sign and date as having reviewed the document.

No problem, as his employee I could to that with him. The problem was that this single page was lined with about forty single bulleted items listed in two different columns on that single page.

As my supervisor tried in earnest to go down through each of these 40 bulleted items and review them with me, he stumbled quite a bit. I didn't want to laugh because the guy was trying his best and was certainly not very experienced, but I kept it all together. I didn't cause any problems for him.

During this review, there was something like one out of every four bulleted items on the first column that he was unclear as to what they meant.

And then when he got to the second column, he just gave up and told me not to worry about them because I was doing a good job so far and would not have any trouble getting a good evaluation when it came time for him to evaluate me.

EMPLOYEE EXPECTATIONS

When he finished, we both signed and dated the document and moved on. What else was there to do?

And as for me, I was not there to establish a career. I was there to do a little research on supervision done in a large retail box store.

Just like in the case study above, my immediate supervisor did not understand the individual employee performance plan document.

He knew it had to be reviewed with me and signed, so the HR would get off his back, but nobody ever took the time to explain the details in the document or how to relate those specific and more general job duties to those employees under his care.

Why would a company, business, agency or any other employer spend the time and effort to create a formal written employee performance evaluation process, and then not make the effort to ensure that the items contained within such documentation were understood by both employee and their immediate supervisor?

The answer to that question is not simple to explain and falls under the category of just being plain fool hearty.

It is my contention that the overwhelming number of employees, including me, want to do a good job. Just tell us what it is you want us to do!!!!

In the 21st century, employers will continue to use some type of formal employee performance evaluation system process complete with formal written employee annual performance plans to measure performance.

In the 21st century, employers will continue to use formal annual written employee plans that are cookie cutter type documents with statements that are written primary to protect the employer during those rare cases when an employee contests a termination.

But having said all of that does not mean that the individual supervisor can't make the whole process more meaningful and successful.

It all starts by taking the time to meet with Human Resources and/or upper management to receive an explanation on each of the items contained in an employee individual performance plan.

It is my contention that all employees will feel much more comfortable supporting their supervisor and their employer if each employee fully understands what is expected of them in their specific employee performance plan. A plan that they are required to sign off on and date as having reviewed and understood with their supervisor as part of the formal employee evaluation process.

It is all part of knowing what their job is.

Summary:

"To Know What Their Job Is."

I have given you four different case studies in this section for your consideration. Just like in Chapter 1, my recommendation is for you to take a moment and reflect how this expectation is being met, or not met, in your workplace.

Again, my guess is that you will be able to make a listing of how the expectation has been, or is currently being, violated in your place of employment.

Do this not to bring attention to the faults of management in your workplace, but do this to give you a reference point in your own setting that you can use as fuel to make improvements in how ***you*** supervise others.

This handbook is a tool for your use to understand and embrace the six employee expectations, but not as a reference to reflect poorly on the management of your organization.

Upper management and the "*worker bees*" will notice and appreciate your commitment to both groups as you continue to strive in terms of meeting employee expectations.

Trust me when I tell you that your adoption and your specific refinement of these principles with make your job as a supervisor more predictable and more enjoyable.

You don't need to pick a fight with upper management simply because not all of your peers or the company leadership have learned the lessons that you are now learning.

Chapter 3- Third Expectation

"To Know When They Are Doing a Good Job."

Of the six employee expectations associated with employee success, this is one of two that seems to be the least understood and addressed; but for totally different reasons.

That other expectation is "To Know When They Are Doing a Poor Job" and will be discussed in the next chapter in detail.

Taking the time to formally and informally recognize good employee performance is an important aspect of successful supervision. All employees want and expect to be told when they are doing a good job.

Expecting praise for doing good work is embedded deeply into the mindset of all employees. This need can be traced back to the time we were all toddlers and sought approval from the adults around us as we learned to accomplish new things or understood some new aspect of the complexities of life in our little world.

That need for approval and acceptance seemed to be one of the major driving factors of our teenage years and in many ways has not diminished as we all matured in adults.

Receiving positive feedback for a job well done as an employee is thus more than simply a nice gesture; it is beyond a shadow of a doubt an employee expectation that is a driving force for employee success in the workplace.

EMPLOYEE EXPECTATIONS

There are many types of employee recognition that can be tailored to a specific workplace, or a specific group of employees, that will satisfy this particular employee expectation and at the same time help to motivate employees to achieve even greater accomplishments.

Please note that often times the type of recognition is not as important as the act of being recognized in a timely and honorable fashion.

Sometimes just a short verbal "job well done" is all that is needed. And sometimes positive recognition for good performance that is more formal and substantial in nature is warranted.

The important point is for the supervisor to recognize good performance when it happens and in a manner consistent with the wishes of the employee and the policies of the organization.

So, let me again be rather poignant.

"It is very common for supervisors to do a poor job in terms of recognizing good employee performance."

I stick by this comment and have seen it time and time again.

This oversight by supervisors is not specific to any type of organization or another. It is simply fact that highly effective and motivating supervisors understand that employees expect to be told (praised) timely for their good performance. Poor supervisors, on the other hand, fail to tell their reports when they are doing a good job.

Why is it that some supervisors fail to recognize the good work of employees?

There are common reasons most often listed by those in supervisory positions for why they do a poor job of recognizing good employee performance:

- I am too busy.
- I don't know how.
- Nobody recognizes me.
- I feel awkward praising good performance.

But I am here to tell you that none of these reasons are valid and should never be a limitation or an excuse for not telling an employee when they are doing a good job.

The following case study offers some insight on the application of employee recognition based on good job performance.

Case Study 3.1 Recognition Frequency.

Nolan had worked as a computer support staff person in the TurnboldQR Manufacturing Co. for six years. During this entire time, he had been instrumental in setting up new computer systems, replacing failing hardware, training new and experience employees on company software applications; and much more.

Bottom line, Nolan was a good, productive and every effective company employee who got along well with his fellow employees.

To Nolan's disappointment, he rarely was recognized, either formally or informally, for the great work he did performing his daily assignments.

EMPLOYEE EXPECTATIONS

He often observed other employees around him that performed different tasks for the company receive recognition many times for the great work they had done over the same period of time, but not Nolan.

But then it happened one day, Nolan's supervisor took the time to recognize his good work. And after his sixth year with the company, Nolan was awarded an outstanding annual performance rating and was then subsequently given a formal letter of recognition, had his picture posted on the company bulletin board in the break room, and received a substantial cash award for his efforts.

Perhaps on the surface, this case study has a happy ending. Nolan's supervisor finally rewarded his work with the highest employee recognition the company could award; and Nolan was such a recipient.

But I am here to tell you that this case study is a tragedy. And that tragedy is all based on the fact that the supervisor did not take into account the magnitude of the expectation that "employees need to know when they are doing a good job."

Even though the supervisor finally came through after six years with such a prestigious performance award, it was *too little too late*.

In this case, Nolan's supervisor simply did not want to be bothered with employee recognition. This supervisor felt that he was too busy to take the time and effort to tell Nolan he was doing a good job. It was recognition enough that Nolan was getting paid every week.

In the supervisor's mind, Nolan's salary was an adequate form of employee recognition for doing a good job.

It was only after six years of consistent and unabated outstanding performance did this particular supervisor finally give the recognition to Nolan that he deserved.

Let me be frank.

In order to meet employee expectations, recognition should come *often*. Employees need and expect positive feedback, and if such feedback is used properly, it can be the strongest motivating factor that a supervisor has at his/her disposal.

In this case, Nolan felt good about this special recognition and at the same time suspected, and rightfully so, that the frequency of being told he was doing a good job would be far and few between.

In some ways, the outstanding annual performance rating made Nolan trust and respect his supervisor even less.

All because no matter how hard Nolan worked, no matter how successful he was completing his assignments, he would likely not get any more positive feedback again, formal or informal, for years under the same supervisor. That was just the way his supervisor operated.

I can also relate to you just how damaging a similar situation was to an employee that I inherited on a short term assignment managing and supervising the administrative section of a large organization.

In this particular administrative section, the former section chief never recognized the good performance of any of the employees under her supervisor. In fact, I had observed this very thing and how she interacted with her reports from afar and considered this behavior rather bizarre and certainly unwise.

On this particular administrative staff was a lady named Alice. Alice was the person in charge of procurement; making sure all of the employees in our large organization had the equipment and supplies needed to do their job.

Alice was very good at negotiating purchases and contracts with private outside vendors. Her negotiating skills thus allowed the organization to save a considerable amount of funds during the procurement process. The direct result was that the company could then use these savings for other uses throughout our business.

In short, she was darn good at what he did. I always wished that I had her as part of my staff. She was that good of an employee.

That year when it came time to for me to review the individual employee yearend performance of the administrative section, I had the opportunity to interact formally with Alice in the supervisor/employee relationship. In doing so, I evaluated her actual performance and accomplishments based on her individual performance plan.

As a result of that review and in concert with my judgment, I made a recommendation that was subsequently approved to award Alice with a yearend performance award similar to the award outlined above for Nolan.

Here is the rest of the story.

The award did not go over well with Alice.

Let me repeat.

"It did not go over well with Alice."

72

Was I shocked?

Yes, I was shocked. Alice came into my office one day after she had received her award with tears in her eyes and was both angry and scared all at the same time.

Why?

Part of it was dealing with a new supervisor that would eventually come, as I was only in a temporary assignment until a new replacement was selected.

But the most compelling reason for her frustration was the fact that Alice was scared to death that she had been awarded such high praise for her performance. She feared that her next supervisor would expect her to do even more than what she was already doing!!!

Alice's concerns were misguided but not without some merit. She was a very hard worker and was very competent at what she did. The lady gave 100%, and then some, each and every day she came to work.

She had never trusted her former supervisor and she was worried now that even 100% plus would not make the grade in the future under her new supervisor.

Ladies and gentlemen.

This is about as strong of evidence that I can provide you of the importance of telling employees when they are doing a good job. And do to so often.

What have should have been a proud and happy moment in Alice's career became a moment of fear. All because of the mismanagement of this expectation in her mind and as administered by her former supervisor.

What happened to Alice?

She eventually calmed down and continued to be the best employee she could each and every day. I can also report to you that her new supervisor understood the importance of "*telling employees when they are doing a good job.*" Alice went on to receive many more outstanding appraisals in her career and she earned each and every one of them.

I know this as a fact because I taught her new supervisor the importance of understanding and taking actions on the six employee expectations outlined in this book.

So how often should a supervisor recognize good employee performance?

Well, that goes hand in hand with timeliness and ties directly into the next case study, but let me say this. Some very highly successful supervisors believe that you should be able to find something good that each employee does every day, or at least weekly and tell them so.

Others say that telling each employee they are doing a good job once every two or three weeks at a minimum is a good target to shoot for.

In fact, I know a supervisor that keeps a written record of when the last time he recognized each of his reports for some aspect of their work that they were doing well on a spread sheet.

He does this in an effort to ensure that he is: LOOKING FOR ANY EXCUSE/REASON TO TELL EVERY EMPLOYEE THEY ARE DOING A GOOD JOB.

It is my opinion that different situations call for difference responses in terms of frequency. The point here is this:

"All employees, each and every one them, will do *something* well from time to time that a

supervisor should recognize as good performance.

The smart supervisor will ensure that such recognition takes place and he/she tells them they are doing a good job.

The how is not as important as the actual act of telling them they are doing a good job."

I know that some readers will be weary of this stance of telling each and every employee they are doing a good job.

But here is the reality.

Each employee is doing at least one aspect of their job rather well, if not, they would not still be employed.

The power of recognizing even the most minor of successes can be a very powerful employee motivating tool.

Why?

Because employees expect to be told when they are doing a good job!!!

But let me be fair and honest with you. Some employees are more challenging to supervise and direct than others, so I came to accept my advice to you by learning it the hard way.

At the beginning, sometimes I had to look long and hard to find any type of good performance for a couple of the knuckleheads that I supervised. But if you take the time to look, you will find that none of your reports are total boneheads at all aspects of their individual job performance.

75

You just need to identify those successes and help the employee channel those successes into more frequent and greater accomplishments.

It is my hope that you will learn from my experiences and simply accept the conclusions as listed in the discussion from the case study, adopt them as your own, and then put those practices to good use.

Timeliness is an important concept in terms of telling employees when they are doing a good job and is subject of the next case study.

Case Study 3.2 Timely Recognition.

Glen and John were both mid level managers in a large national organization we will call OregonXZ Rat Traps.

In most organizations, and as happens from time to time, a major crisis will arise that needs to be addressed. That is just the nature of doing business. Stuff happens. Most often such a crisis will become the immediate and the top priority of the organization. Such was the case for OregonXZ Rat Traps.

During a scheduled financial accounting review of OregonXZ Rat Traps, the outside accounting firm the organization used discovered that the contracts being written with clients by company officials all across the country, in nearly every office, were deficient. These contracts would not be defensible under current federal and state tax laws; particularly since there was federal funding involved in these contracts and could be seen as violations of federal appropriation laws.

As a direct result of the accounting deficiencies, Glen and John, along with many others in the company, were called into the national headquarters and provided training on how to fix the contracts. The training was intense and each participant came away with a clear understanding in terms of how to correct the contract deficiencies. The urgency of such corrections was also made clear. It was the top priority of the organization and there was a deadline established. Nothing was deemed more important.

When Glen and John came back to their region, they immediately went to work training contract writers on the policies and directions that needed to be followed in order to develop appropriate new contracts. In addition, they provided instructions on how to go back and correct existing contracts.

Then to top it all off, Glen and John became the contract development quality control experts for OregonXZ Rat Traps for their region.

Because of the nature of this self made company crisis, Glen and John spent the next six months successfully addressing the associated issues. In doing so, they went above and beyond and worked many extra hours day after day traveling from office to office.

The end result of their efforts was that OregonXZ Rat Traps successfully corrected 100% of the deficient contracts, plus 100% of all newly developed contracts met the new standards consistent with the new company policies and in line with the recommendations of the outside financial audit.

77

All of this success was a direct result of the efforts and leadership provided by Glen and John in their region of the country through the specific course of action that they had taken.

It wasn't until eight (8) months after Glen and John completed this assignment to address what became the number one priority assignment for all offices of OregonXZ Rat Traps, that these two employees were told they had done a good job addressing the financial deficiencies for their region.

That recognition came in the form of a simple coin specialty made with the company logo on it to recognize those that went above and beyond the normal call of duty to address the contracting issues.

Nothing more was said. The coins were simply sent to Glen and John in the mail. The crisis was over.

It could be argued that the type of recognition that these two employees received from their employee did not mesh with the magnitude of what they accomplished. And to be fair; I would agree with you, but let's save that discussion for later. What I want to focus on here is the timeliness of the award.

If I am doing an acceptable level of outlining this case study to you, it should be apparent that this financial crisis was serious to the continued welfare of OregonXZ Rat Traps and how they did business. They had to get this right.

Glen and John both went out of their way to work nights and weekends to assist the company recover from these known contract deficiencies. It was important work.

78

It was time sensitive work. Failure was not an option. And most importantly, Glen and John performed well and fixed the mess.

One would have thought that this national company would have jumped up and down for joy at the actions of these two employees and would have went out of their way to show appreciation for a job well done.

But it did not happen until many months later.

I can tell you this much. These two employees were shocked and disappointed. The crisis was now in the past and everyone went back to their normal duties and nothing more was said. No atta/boys. Nothing.

In reality, and what can happen in many organizations once a crisis is over, the company leadership moves on and passes the "pat on the back" process to Human Resources (HR) or some other entity within the organization

In this case, HR was not sure how to recognize the Glens and Johns of OregonXZ Rat Traps for a job well done. The accomplishments of employees like Glen and John was certainly noteworthy and deserved special attention, but what?

So the end result was that HR dragged their heels week after week and month after month, until they came up with a unique method to say thank you for a job well done to employees like Glen and John.

HR decided to have a one-time commemorative company coin minted to honor those who had gone above and beyond to fix the financial crisis.

The problem with all of this was the fact that once the decision was made on how to say "*good job*" and thank the Glens and Johns of the company, it took another three months to have these same one-time commemorative coins minted and sent out.

EMPLOYEE EXPECTATIONS

I can share this much with you as well. Both Glen and John were good and sound OregonXZ Rat Traps employees but their pride was damaged when their company never recognized the good work they had done during the crisis.

Nothing informal, and nothing formal.

When the two coins arrived, which were meant to be a significant and cherished reward for Glen and John for all of their hard work, neither employee gave a damn.

Glen took one look as his newly minted coin, laughed and then tossed it a drawer.

John laughed, shook his head and then promptly gave it away to the first employee he saw as a souvenir.

Nothing more was said.

Let me be clear, Glen and John were not ungrateful employees. But receiving recognition for a job well done eight (8) months after the fact is an insult. The crisis was long gone and forgotten about for the most.

The significance of their work and their accomplishments now seemed somewhat diminished. OregonXZ Rat Traps did not fully appreciate the fact that employees expect:

"To Know When They Are Doing a Good Job."

For recognition to be meaningful, *__it has to be timely__*. This is a fundamental and important aspect of telling employees when they are doing a good job. It is the supervisor's job to see to it that both formal and informal recognition are done in a timely fashion.

If you see an employee doing something well and you are impressed, tell them right then and there. Don't wait and come back to it later.

You want to reward good work with positive reinforcement at the time it happens, or at least as soon as possible thereafter.

Let me give you a positive example of what is meant here.

Have you ever seen how the successful NFL football coach Pete Caroll works with his players during a game?

If a player makes a good play, whether it is the kicker kicking a field goal, a linebacker intercepting a pass, or a receiver catching a pass for a touchdown and those same players are leaving the field after the play, Coach Caroll personally walks over to that player and pats him on the back right during the game. He doesn't wait until the next day, next week or sometime later. He congratulates their excellent play right then and there.

Why?

Because he knows that giving congratulations for good execution is not as meaningful or effective later on and loses some of the impact.

He recognizes this fact and doesn't want the accomplishment to lose some of the luster with his positive feedback later on seeming like just and an afterthought.

He also has come to understand that the best way to encourage more of the same good performance from his players in the future is to reward good play at the time it all happens. That is when it is most effective and there is no confusion as to what the coach conceives as good play.

The same kind of thing is true in all workplaces.

There is an old saying that goes something like this:

"There is no better time than the present."

Recognizing good performance, in a timely fashion, is very important beyond a shadow of a doubt. Highly successful supervisors understand this concept very well.

In this chapter thus far we have sort of danced around the issue of how to recognize good performance. The following case study features a brief discussion on that aspect of employee recognition for doing a good job.

Case Study 3.3 How to Recognize.

Taylor was a law partner in a large size law firm in the Silicon Valley in California that processed patents for many tech companies on the West Coast.

To be sure, Taylor was not an extrovert and had chosen to study electrical engineering at the prestigious Iowa State University. Most of the people that interacted with her, either professionally or socially, knew her as the quiet non-assuming type.

In her field of law, she mostly worked with other techies in the world of patent law. She never had to go to court and did most of her law practice parked behind a computer writing patents.

But in her role as a partner in the firm, she supervised and provided direction to a whole "flock" of associates and interns processing patents under her direction for her clients.

82

Coming up through the ranks and into her current position as a law partner, Taylor did not receive a lot of positive feedback from the senior law partners about her job performance.

There were no awards. No informal *"atta/girls."* Just an annual cash bonus that was awarded to her and every other associate at the end of the business year. It seemed like the amount of the dollar award was directly tied to the number of hours she actually billed to clients.

So when she became a partner and had associates working directly for her, she had no first-hand experience to follow in terms of telling her reports when they were doing a good job. She did not know any better.

Interacting with employees as a supervisor was not something taught to her in the engineering department at Iowa State or at her law school in southern California.

In her mind, since the only positive feedback she got coming up through the system was simply the amount of the cash bonus at the end of the year, she thus considered that the awarding of the cash bonus was all she needed to do.

My experience is that lawyers and law firms are a pathetic social experiment that somehow went awry. I am still amazed that to this day, there are absolutely no constitutional requirements to be appointed to the Supreme Court of the United States of America!!!
None.

EMPLOYEE EXPECTATIONS

Now I can understand that in 1787 when the constitution was being formulated that under those circumstances that it was very likely that there was a shortage of good lawyers; just based on the history and the lack of formal educational opportunities at the time.

And I guess there still must be a shortage of good lawyers even today and that is why there are still no constitutional requirements to serve as a Supreme Court Justice. Go figure.

Poking fun at lawyers obviously is not the issue of this case study. All of us as citizens have to deal with lawyers in one way or another everyday of our life. For when our learned friends fail at their chosen vocation, they run for public office. I mean what else are they going to do?

The real nugget of wisdom to pass on here is that even in organizations, where the majority of people are highly educated professionals; it is very common to have supervisors that are often clueless about how to recognize employees when they do good work.

And since these same individuals themselves never received the positive reinforcement and recognition for their work related accomplishments, why should their employees expect anything different.

This attitude of "*I didn't get any, and so I'm not going to give any,* "is far more prevalent in the workplace than most business leaders want to acknowledge.

We have all seen this attitude. I have. You have. We all have and in every type of workplace in this country.

Remember, employees expect to be told when they are doing a good job. And when that never happens, or happens so seldom that it really doesn't matter, employee expectations are not being met and there is a certain level of dissatisfaction that then fosters.

Sure, it does take an effort for a supervisor to tell an employee that they are doing a good job. But here is another little secret, the more a supervisor tells their employees they are doing a good job, the easier it gets for that supervisor to do that very thing.

I can almost assure you that when NFL head coach Pete Caroll takes the time to praise good efforts by his players, he doesn't even have to think about. It now just comes naturally to him, and it can come naturally to you as well.

No matter how poorly or infrequently, in terms of receiving acknowledgment for doing a good job by a past or current supervisor, that personal experience should not cloud a supervisor's judgment or responsibility to recognize good performance from their reports.

And then to the claim that supervisors just don't know how to tell employees when they are doing a good job is also unacceptable.

Knowing how to tell employees when they are doing a good job is certainly a fixable training item.

Informal Recognition

Informal recognition and acknowledgment of a job well done can take on many forms.

The on-the-spot recognition is the most common and in many ways the most effective way to tell an employee that they are doing a good job.

If you "*catch*" an employee doing something of note, walk up to them and tell them they are doing a good job. It is not that difficult to do. It just needs to be sincere, and is best accomplished by being somewhat specific.

EMPLOYEE EXPECTATIONS

Marvin observes that an employee named Sally under his supervision is going a great job of keeping the shelves in the cooler fully stocked with milk for the customer rush that comes during the late afternoon hours between 4-6 p.m. It is during this time period when the largest volume of milk is sold to customers that stop by the store on their way home after work.

In this scenario, Marvin could:

1. Do nothing and walk on by because that is what the employee is paid to do.
2. He could stop and say, *"Doing good work there, Sally."*
3. He could stop and say, *"Great job Sally keeping the milk shelves full. The next two hours are always the busiest for selling milk."*

In the supervisory training that I provide to others, I would encourage them to do something along the lines of option #3.

Why?

Because you do not want to leave any doubt or confusion with the employee as to why you are congratulating them on a job well done.

I have seen and heard supervisors tell employees that they are doing good work and then these same employees turn to a cohort who heard the comment and ask the other employee:

"What did I do?"

"I don't know but whatever it is, you might want to keep it up.

Again the employee expectation is to be told when they are doing a good job. You don't want there to be any confusion, if you can help it.

Maybe the next time this particular supervisor catches Sally doing a good job or keeping the milk cooler fully stocked, he could simply say while pointing at the milk shelves: "Doing good work there, Sally."

There are many other options for informal ways that a supervisor can tell an employee that they are doing a good job. Doing a quick search on the internet can yield a whole selection of different ideas to choose from.

Your role is to find ways to adopt some of these suggestions that fit into your style of management and the culture of your organization.

Besides the on-the-spot thank you used to tell an employee that they are doing a good job, my second favorite method of recognizing good performance is through the awarding of "*keepsake awards*."

I once worked for a large organization that allocated funds each year to purchase company keepsake awards for distribution by senior level supervisors for reports under their direction.

The rules associated with the awarding of keepsake awards were straightforward and simple.

1. **No formal paperwork was required.**
2. **All employees eligible to receive keepsake awards.**
3. **Awards were to be timely.**
4. **These supervisors maintained direct access to a whole collection of keepsake items.**

5. **The decision to make awards rested with these supervisors, not with HR or upper management.**
6. **Supervisors should look for reasons to award good work.**
7. **No limit on number awards issued.**

For this particular organization, keepsake items consisted of things like: watches, desk clocks, different items of clothing apparel, umbrellas, pen and pencil sets, ice chests and coolers, coffee mugs; etc.

Each one of these keepsake awards were marked or labeled with the company logo. And I can tell you this much, employees proudly wore their keepsake shirts, coats, and hats both at work and away from work.

In a way, these keepsake awards also helped to foster unity and pride in the organization that we all worked for and such benefits should not be understated.

I remember one time that I awarded a keepsake award to an employee who did not work for my company but worked for another organization that we partnered with.

This employee was totally shocked but very appreciative of receiving this keepsake award for the partnership work he completed with my organization.

He had been working for his organization for over 25 years and had never received any type of award for his efforts. And this particular man was a very respected and accomplished employee. Sort of gives you an idea of the impact of awarding a simple informal award in the from a keepsake item.

Let me sum up this section by listing four simple informal methods from a whole laundry list of options that can be adopted and used to tell an employee that they are going a good job.

From my experience, these four methods have a proven track record of being very effective:

1. **On-the-spot "atta boy/atta girl."**
2. **Hand written thank you notes.**
3. **Have the big boss come by and say "Great Job."**
4. **Keepsake awards.**

The number three (3) item listed above is more powerful than most supervisors and managers can even imagine. A simple pat on the back for good work by the big boss himself/herself is a **VERY BIG DEAL**.

I have never seen a single time when such an effort wasn't greatly appreciated by an employee. In some ways, it is most humbling.

And when such high praise as simple as this takes place, I can guarantee that the affected employee will go home that day and report the event to their family and/or friends. That is a fact you can take to the bank. Nothing is better that the positive attention from the big boss.

The flip side is this. The big boss will be humbled as well afterwards.

For the most part, the big boss rarely fully appreciates the impact that they can have on employee morale and engagement.

It is your job to make sure that every once in a while you get the big boss out on their office to simply tell an employee, or a set of employees, that they appreciate the good work your reports are doing for the organization.

EMPLOYEE EXPECTATIONS

This is a point that you don't want to forget. Don't let anybody talk you out of using the "big boss" to pat the back of one of the employees under your direction and care for doing a good job!!!!

Formal Recognition

Just like informal recognition, formal recognition used to acknowledge a job well done, can take on many forms.

It all depends on the management/employee interaction and how that interaction is realized in the culture and the environment of a specific organization.

Formal recognition usually requires a concerted effort on the immediate supervisor to carry out and administer.

Often such efforts include completing required paperwork in a timely fashion that is formatted specifically to the policies of the organization. As such, each and every supervisor must to be committed to the process in order to properly follow company policies and the filing of the necessary paperwork.

If a supervisor is not familiar, or does not understand the policies and procedures associated with the roles they play in administering formal recognition for their employees, THOSE SUPERVISORS NEED TO FIGURE IT OUT. Not tomorrow. Not the next day. But now, today.

From my experience, it does take a certain amount of effort again for each supervisor to fully understand the nuisances of any formal employee recognition program. These formal award programs have award criteria that must be met before an individual or group employee award recommendation can be approved.

It is just the nature of the beast, and for good reason.

Formal awards are most often handed out for more significant accomplishments and generally comprise substantial investments by the organization used to praise, thank, and encourage superior or outstanding job performance.

Formal awards are thus usually reserved for those employees that went far and above the normal call of duty; and not reserved for efforts made to meet the minimal standards of any specific job.

Simply stated, formal awards are usually reserved for exceptional job performance and warrant special recognition. Such recognition often times will include monetary and other types of acknowledgement that will be a direct cost, or a direct investment depending on your point of view, to the organization.

And just like reviewing different options for informal recognition, an internet review can yield many suggestions on how to more formally recognize good job performance.

Below is a listing of some of the common forms of formal recognition but is by no means exhaustive of the different options available; or other forms that could be developed for situations unique to each organization.

- Letters of Appreciation
- Certificates of Merit
- Plaques
- Cash Awards
- Time off Awards
- Promotions
- Salary Increases; etc

EMPLOYEE EXPECTATIONS

As I reported above, it does take an effort for each supervisor to complete the paperwork or other requirements to recommend an employee for a formal award.

The good news is that most HR managers will take the time to help a supervisor to understand the procedures required if such assistance is sought out.

If not, work with a fellow supervisor that understands the nuisances of the formal award system to obtain a grasp of what hoops need to be jumped through in order for you to be successful.

If, as a supervisor, you are committed to the expectation that employees need to be told when they are doing a good job, you will humble yourself enough to learn the organization's award program. Even if you have to learn the system on your own time, I would advise you to do it.

I can tell you this much.

The more experience you have with the administration of the formal employee awards program for your organization, the easier it will become.

I can also tell you that as you work to gain such experience, you will likely make some mistakes in the process of justifying and documenting formal awards, but those mistakes can be correctable. It just takes an effort from you as the supervisor.

I will also tell you that an HR staff person, or some other entity, may require that you redo an award documentation that they deem is inadequate. When this happens, take the time to fix any deficiencies in your documentation. It is what your reports would expect you to do.

Another trick to remember is that as you are learning the system ask HR for positive written examples of adequate documentation that you can use as a guide to help you through the process. Most HR types will support that idea. After all, they are not in the business of wanting to hassle with you over award recommendations. It is just that they have a job to do and so do you. Treat them as a resource that can help you through the process.

Now please don't get the wrong idea. I have seen supervisors just dump a mess on the desk of an HR staffer and hope they will accept it and fix the deficiencies in terms of award documentation that they submitted. That approach is never a good idea and your employees will suffer for your laziness.

In my career, I have seen award recommendation after award recommendation simply denied because the required documentation was not provided by the immediate supervisor. Sometimes the supervisor would make the needed changes, and sometimes they would not and just forget it. The employee then suffers.

So if you need to redo your documentation over and over again until you get it right, just do it. After a while, it will all make sense to you. That is a promise. I have been on both sides of this issue.

Here is an undeniable and powerful fact about formal employee recognition:

"Employees prefer to work for, and with, supervisors that are committed to recognize good job performance for employees under their care."

93

EMPLOYEE EXPECTATIONS

Below is the next and final case study focusing on the employee expectation of being told when they are doing a good job.

Case Study 3.4. Recognize When Perfect.

Jody was supervised by a veteran supervisor named Warren who had worked for nearly twenty years at the HarringtonTL Construction and Demolition Co in southwest Texas.

Warren was a supportive supervisor for the most part, but he was a perfectionist. Whether it was his engineering background, his military background or his insecurities supervising others, he would not tell an employee when they were doing a good job unless everything was perfect.

The end result was that Warren was a supervisor that rarely rated his employees above average. He wanted perfection and everything else was just something less.

It was his feeling that performance recognition, formal or informal, came only after perfection was reached, and not until.

Really?

Warren was wrong. Warren was an idiot. Warren may not have what it takes to supervise and provide direction to others. Here is why.

Nobody is perfect. Nobody.

The expectations that Warren had for his employees was not realistic. While it is true that quality, quantity, timeliness; etc are important aspects of any

94

engineering or construction business, nothing in the construction field is ever perfect. I get that and so should Warren. Stuff happens.

I have supervised many engineers over the years and from a general standpoint, engineers are way too hard on employees they supervise.

The HarringtonTL Construction and Demolition Co was, and is, a very successful construction firm with a great reputation. They do great work, period.

How did they achieve such success?

They did so with the help of a whole "flock" of good competent employees.

It should never be the personal policy of an individual supervisor to never recognize good employee job performance until everything is perfect. Such a policy is not consistent with using positive reinforcement concerning employee job performance.

If the company is so successful, those employees under Warren's supervision must be doing something right, and he should be recognizing them for it.

The reason I added the case study with Warren here for discussion is really twofold.

First. **Never wait until an employee does their job perfect before you decide to let them know they are doing a good job.**

Second. **It is never too late as a supervisor to make adjustments in how you supervise.**

Once it was brought to his attention that he was expecting too much in terms of perfection, Warren learned to better appreciate the employees he worked with and became a more supportive supervisor.

There was a learning curve, but he did learn how to tell employees when they were doing a good job through both formal and informal recognition. And to be truthful, he still has a way to go but he is getting there.

So, I take it all back. Warren is not an idiot. Warren is trainable and is making the necessary adjustments he needs to make in order to become a highly successful supervisor.

He has my support.

Summary:

"To Know When They Are Doing a Good Job."

Telling employees when they are doing a good job and recognizing their contributions to the success of the organization should come naturally to all supervisors. But the sad truth is that it doesn't, and some supervisors are simply horrible at praising employees for their accomplishments.

The excuse that a supervisor doesn't have the time is pitiful. I mean woefully pitiful. In every single work environment that I have been a part of, the highly successful supervisors have found the time to tell employees when they are doing a good job.

The excuse that the supervisor doesn't know how is just as pitiful. That is because every supervisor has resources available to assist in the process. Assistance could be provided by HR, or from a peer that knows the company awards program and can provide guidance to navigate through the procedures leading to success.

The excuse that nobody recognizes me or I feel awkward praising good performance are in many ways the most pitiful excuses of all.

Telling employees when they are doing good is NOT about the supervisor. It is about the employee they supervise!!!

Whether or not the supervisor is ever recognized for good performance is irrelevant. There may be some very concrete reasons for that lack of recognition.

In fact, the point that the supervisor never tells their own reports when they are doing a good job is in my mind a direct indication that the supervisor is in fact a poor supervisor.

Not recognizing the good work of employees is a definite "red flag" to the lack of competence of a given supervisor. Such a lack of supervisor support will not go unnoticed forever and will lead to employee dissatisfaction and high turnover.

Again, take a moment and reflect on how this expectation is, or is not, being met in your workplace. And then take those observations and use them to develop a plan on how you can make improvements in your own supervisory role.

In the **Case Study 3.2, Timely Recognition**, Glen and John performed exceptionally well under some difficult and time sensitive circumstances. The recognition they eventually received for their efforts came in the form of a commemorative coin with the company logo minted on the coin.

Was this recognition commensurate with the degree of their extra efforts?

I would argue that it was not, and this is an important point about formal and informal recognition.

EMPLOYEE EXPECTATIONS

The type and extent of the recognition should fit the degree of the accomplishment.

Truly over the top extra efforts should not be awarded the same as simple routine day to day small successes. Such extra efforts deserve a higher degree of recognition.

And then small accomplishments should not be rewarded with lavish praise, cash, and other compensations.

Trust me when I tell you this, employees will know the difference and when they are being "cheated" in terms of the kind of recognition they receive. If the level of the award doesn't mesh with the level of accomplishment, employee dissatisfaction will take place.

In this case study, Glen and John expected some type of monetary compensation for their "herculean" efforts.

Such compensation was very common in their organization for those employees that went above and beyond their normal duties. And when that compensation did not happen, they felt betrayed and unappreciated.

These two employee were both salaried employees and all of the extra hours they put into the effort did not mean any increase in their salary. There was an increase in work and duties that far exceeded normal 40 hour work weeks, but there was not an increase in salary. No overtime pay. Nothing.

Again, I have also witnessed situations that are the polar opposite of this case study. Situations where employees received awards and financial compensations for efforts that really weren't all that significant.

The point is to ensure that the type and amount of any formal recognition appropriately fits the level and significance of the accomplishment obtained and efforts provided. That is what employees expect.

It is extremely important and vital to the success of any organization for supervisors to tell employees when they are doing a good job.

It is also extremely important for a supervisor to understand and use the administrative tools at their disposal to recognize good job performance using both informal and formal measures within the acceptable policies and culture of the organization.

Chapter 4- Fourth Expectation

"To Know When They Are Doing a Poor Job."

Of the six employee expectations associated with employee success, this is the second of two that seems to be the least understood and addressed. The other expectation, "To Know When They Are Doing a Good Job," was discussed in Chapter 3; and in some ways goes hand in hand with "To Know When They Are Doing a Poor Job."

It is the flip side of the coin and is a symbol of how closely related these two expectations really are. You can't have one without the other because none of us do everything perfectly. We employees just need a little feedback to keep us on the right track.

As I have outlined before, one of the lessons that I have learned over the years is just how important it is for each supervisor to strive to meet all of the employee expectations for every single employee under their direction.

However, it has been my observation that many supervisors just try to skirt around this one. The reasons for this attitude vary but are usually tied to the simple fact that supervisors don't want to be the *"bad"* guy.

Telling an employee when and how they are performing poorly is often seen as controversial and fraught with tension.

The end result is that supervisors just hope somehow that their reports will figure it all out and make the needed adjustments on their own.

100

Or in some cases, the supervisor will continue to avoid telling an employee when they are doing a poor job until the situation has deteriorated to the point that discussions with HR are made concerning employee termination.

My thinking is that leading and directing employees doesn't have to tension filled; especially as it is related to this specific expectation.

My thinking is that supervisors are just not looking logically at the VALUE TO THE EMPLOYEE of letting them know when they are doing a poor job.

Why?

Because the overwhelming majority of employees WANT to do a good job. Let me repeat that:

"THE OVERWHELMING MAJORITY OF EMPLOYEES WANT TO DO A GOOD JOB."

They **WANT** to do a good job!!!
They **NEED** to be able to do a good job!!!
They **EXPECT** that they can do a good job!!!

Job related employee self worth and job satisfaction are directly interlaced with this feeling of:

I CAN DO this job.
And **I CAN DO IT WELL.**

One of the keys components for employee success is then tied directly to knowing when they are not performing their job well so they can make the needed adjustments to succeed.

101

Now to be clear, I am not talking about beating down an employee. I am not talking about belittling an employee. I am not talking about insulting the dignity of an employee.

What I am talking about is giving employee constructive feedback. Feedback that will make it clear where and how to make corrections in job performance that can directly lead to greater success and enhance the opportunities for employees.

This first case study addresses the fact that often employees don't understand or appreciate when they are NOT performing well because nobody let them know.

Case Study 4.1 Engineering Failure

In one of my past roles, I was supervising 14 different units. Each unit had a supervisor that was one of my direct reports. And under each of those supervisors was a staff of employees with various occupational series who were valued team members of the organization that we all worked for.

One of my direct reports was a supervisor named Rich. Rich had an employee named Kathy under his care that was in a training program and was in her probationary period within the organization.

Rich had called me and we were discussing Kathy's progress in the training program. As such, Rich noted that there was one aspect of the job that Kathy was not progressing very well, engineering.

In fact, Kathy had indicated to Dave and others that she did not like engineering and would just as soon

102

leave that aspect of her job to somebody else. Her skills in surveying were not progressing very well and her design skills and understanding of basic engineering standards were not improving either.

When I asked Rich if he had a discussion with Kathy about the duties of her training position and that being competent in engineering was a key component of the job, he was rather quiet.

But with some prodding, Rich finally informed me that he didn't know how to tell her that. He didn't want to upset her and tell her she was failing in this important aspect of her position. He hated to see women cry and he sensed that if he told her she was doing something wrong, she would shed come tears. Men were just easier to work with is what he then told me.

During our discussion, I eventually asked Rich if he recommended terminating Kathy while she was still in the probationary period. If Kathy was doing such a poor job with engineering, then why not just release her?

Rich said that he did not know what he would recommend, whether to keep her on as a full-time permanent employee, or to release her. He just hoped that maybe given some time, she would show some improvement.

This case study is fraught with important lessons to be discussed about how to be a highly successful supervisor. But first let me begin by addressing employee expectations that a new employee like Kathy has during her probationary period.

It is extremely important that the Kathy's of the world understand what their job is, and what it is not, as already outlined earlier in this text.

In this case, Kathy understood that engineering was part of her new job but she was not given any feedback just how important that part of her job really was. Her direct supervisor failed to provide her with any feedback that her engineering skills were not improving and that if this continued, her employment with the organization would not continue.

Without a doubt, Rich was failing Kathy as her direct supervisor. He knew that her job performance in terms of engineering was not up to standards, but he felt uncomfortable correcting her and holding her accountable. Doing so was just too controversial and he wanted to avoid that type of conflict.

Rich was missing the point.

All employees expect to be informed when they are doing a poor job, Kathy included.

The overwhelming number of employees "*want*" *to do a good job*.

The overwhelming numbers of employees "*need*" to be able to do a good job.

The overwhelming numbers of employees "expect" that they can do a good job.

Bottom line, and to make sure that both Rich and Kathy understood that for her to be successful, Kathy would need to demonstrate that she could handle the rigors of all aspects of her position to include engineering, I invited them both into my office to discuss her progress as a trainee.

During this informal meeting, I did most of the talking and interaction with Kathy. We talked about her progress concerning all aspects of her position to include the engineering aspects that she was essentially failing at.

Kathy was unaware that her job performance was subpar in terms of the engineering aspects; and that for her to survive her probationary period she would have to show marked improvement.

She further admitted that she did not like engineering but thought that she could learn what she needed to know and could be successful in the future.

To be truthful, the conversations caught both Rich and Kathy red faced. Both realized that they had let each other down in the realm of supervisor/employee interactions.

And to be honest, Kathy did shed a tear of two after I outlined in some detail her unsatisfactory job performance in detail in terms of how she was performing her engineering duties, but that is not how the discussion ended.

Before this meeting concluded on that day, and together as a team, we outlined future training needs for Kathy to provide her direct and immediate feedback as she continued in her training position. She would work towards becoming competent in all aspects of her position; with a strong emphasis on the engineering components under the supervision and direction of Rich.

EMPLOYEE EXPECTATIONS

The rest of the story is this.

Kathy made a complete 180 degree turn around in her job performance, not only in engineering but in all aspects of her position. She made it through her probationary period just fine and was recommended to be retained as a permanent hire.

I am also proud to say that Kathy went on to become a successful manager within the organization. Today, she is a vital cog and respected employee by all levels of management inside the organization.

This case study, which focuses on a single snapshot in her career, highlights the value of telling employees when they are doing a poor job so that they can have the chance to make the needed adjustments.

I can tell you that the immediate result of our discussion was that both Kathy and Rich were happier employees.

Kathy and Rich learned important lessons on employee expectations, and Kathy took this particular lesson with her into her future role as a supervisor of others.

In my mind, the situation with Kathy simply dragged out far too long. All Rich had to do was inform Kathy where her performance was deficient and outline what she needed to do in order to improve.

It is all about timing and the best time to inform an employee when they are not doing a good job is the first time it comes to the attention of the supervisor.

"Nip poor job performance in the bud before the situation gets out of hand."

And then this whole issue of Rich not wanting to confront Kathy because she was a woman is just hogwash.

How can any employee, man or woman, make the necessary corrections in how they perform their job if nobody outlines to them when they are doing a poor job?

Not to inform employees when they are "*screwing*" up is simply not responsible and is unfair both to the employee and the employer.

The U.S. Secretary of Defense has now determined that women can serve in direct combat roles right alongside their male counterparts. There is a point to be made with that determination.

It is my experience, and my contention, that to underestimate a woman employee's resolve, maturity, and abilities based on her sex is a terrible mistake and a waste of talent.

Look, my mother is only 4' 10.5" tall, and you would be hard pressed to find a tougher more determined individual all packed into the tiny frame that is my mother. She can handle herself in the business world, and so could Kathy.

Rich using the excuse that he didn't want to tell Kathy that she was doing a poor job because he didn't want to see her cry was just plain hogwash as well. That was an excuse. Nothing more. Nothing less.

In reality Rich, as Kathy's supervisor, had failed yet to embrace the fact that all employees **EXPECT TO BE TOLD WHEN THEY ARE DOING A POOR JOB** so that they can have the opportunity to make the needed corrections.

An employee can't make corrections if they don't know what they're doing is wrong. It is that simple, and it is that straightforward.

EMPLOYEE EXPECTATIONS

This next case study highlights the value of experience and using experience to assist employees make corrections in how they do their jobs.

Case Study 4.2 Hit the Ball.

Jose Bacon was once the number one draft choice of the major league ball club, the Springfield Lions. He was now in his fourth year in the minors and had become a disappointment to the ball club because his hitting skills had not progressed enough to be assigned to the big club. Jose was still stuck in the minors and seemed to be heading nowhere but out of baseball.

It was not that Jose wasn't making a concerted effort to improve his hitting skills, because he worked harder that anyone in the organization. But no matter how hard he tried; his hitting skills seemed to be getting worse and not better.

Jose Bacon was at the end of his rope and his dream of playing major league baseball was in the balance. He did not know why he couldn't hit. He had tried everything he could think of to do to improve his hitting.

It was about this time in his career that Jose got a new hitting coach. This new coach looked at the stance Jose had in the box, his swing from beginning to the follow through, his approach to different pitches; etc.

This coach was able to point out what Jose was doing wrong and why it was predictable that he couldn't hit the pitching of a big league pitcher. The

new coach also outlined what steps Jose could take to be more successful.

The results were amazing. Jose improved his hitting skills all because his new hitting coach explained to him what he was doing wrong and Jose accepted that advice from an experienced hitting coach.

All of us that follow baseball, at any level, can relate to this story. Baseball is a difficult sport with so many different aspects to the game that get more refined as a player climbs up the skill ladder of organized baseball. It is the reason that so very few ball players make it to the major leagues.

I have a cousin who was the number one draft choice of a MLB team that will remain nameless, but sounds like the St. Louis Cardinals. This kid was left handed and was an outstanding high school pitcher growing up in California. But having success in high school did not guarantee his success in the professional baseball much in a manor quite similar to the story with Jose as outlined above.

It wasn't until my cousin, with the help of a professional pitching staff, figured how what he was doing wrong, that enabled him to succeed in the major leagues for three different ball clubs over his career.

The point of the baseball case study is the recognition of player shortcomings and then addressing those shortcomings.

If you are a sports fan, you know that big money is spent telling professional athletes what they are doing wrong, and then assisting them in making the necessary adjustments. Just look at how many coaches make up a professional baseball or football team.

In fact, I once heard a rumor that there were so many coaches in the NFL that the Commissioner was thinking about putting out a contract to "spray" for the coaches.

Well, maybe I just made that up.

But if we can see how important it is to tell a professional athlete when they are doing a poor job; and then give those athletes a chance to correct those deficiencies, then supervisors in any organization should be able to perceive the same value of informing employees when they are doing a poor job.

The following case study relates to a situation that is very common in the workplace where employees have direct contact with the customers/clients.

Case Study 4.3 Service to Customers/Clients.

Peddle, Sell & Save is a big box retail chain with local stores located all across the country. At one particular store, located in a midsize city in the Midwest, there worked an employee named Marvin. Marvin was a part-time employee that had been working for only about four weeks.

His main duty was to stock shelves in the produce section which was a high volume part of the store. As a new employee trying to learn his job and keep up with the demands of stocking shelves, he was failing at an important aspect of his position, customer service.

When a customer stopped him and asked the location of a product outside of the produce section, Marvin often wasn't sure and would simply point the customer in the direction where he best guessed the product was located, and then went about his business.

Sometimes, he guessed right and sent the customer in the right direction; and sometimes he guessed wrong and sent the customer on a wild goose chase to the opposite end of the store.

This type of interaction had happened nearly every day during Marvin's brief tenure at Peddle, Sell & Save. Sometimes a customer would tell another employee that the guy in produce did not seem to know anything, but the word never got passed back to Marvin that his customer service skills were not up to par.

Even though he was good at keeping the produce shelves stocked it was obvious to other store employees that Marvin did not interact with customers very well.

One day it all caught up to Marvin when after he sent a customer on a wild goose chase, that customer complained to store management that Marvin had not been very helpful, and that he didn't seem to know where things were located in the very store where he worked. That particular customer had been very vocal in the complaint.

The subsequent result was that the Peddle, Sell & Save manager chased Marvin down in the store and

reprimanded him for not helping that customer find the product that she was looking for.

In this case study, there are several issues to deal with including teamwork, or lack thereof; misunderstanding of the scope of the job; and not informing Marvin when he was doing a poor job so that he could make the needed corrections.

As a new employee and trying his best to keep up with the constant demands of keeping the produce shelves stocked, Marvin did not have time to wonder around the store and become more familiar with the location of various products.

That was simply not part of the training that he had been provided and he thus figured that customer service and helping customers locate product must not have been all that important for him in his new position.

In his mind, he was supposed to keep the shelves stocked and answer customer questions dealing with his little "produce world" inside the store as a whole.

This case study or something similar happens a lot in large stores with a large inventory and variety of products and services that are for sale.

New employees simply are not that familiar with where all products are located and they aren't sure how far they are to go to help customers in the search for a product.

In this case study, seasoned employees had a sense that Marvin was struggling with this aspect of his job. Yet nobody stepped in and informed him that he was doing a poor job assisting customers find product items and that customer service was a major job responsibility of all employees.

None of these same seasoned employees explained to Marvin that if he did not know the location of a product and there was a customer inquiry, he could simply get on his walkie-talkie and ask where the product was located. Someone would let him know exactly where the product was located by responding back to him through the walkie-talkie.

Even Marvin's direct supervisor had reason to believe that Marvin was failing at assisting customers find products, and yet that same supervisor had just let things go.

It wasn't until store management was confronted by an irate customer did somebody finally tell Marvin that he was doing a poor job with customer service.

This situation was really not Marvin's fault.

If management wanted him to be more proactive in helping all customers with product questions than the methods he was using, all they had to do was to provide him with feedback.

Marvin thought his performance was in line with what he thought was required of him. He thought he was doing just fine keeping the produce section stocked.

All his supervisor had to do was to be upfront and honest with Marvin by providing him the necessary feedback so that Marvin could be successful.

Below are some examples of feedback that could have been used by the supervisor to deal with this issue:

1. "Marvin, when a customer asks about the location of a product, and you don't know where the product is located in the store, don't send them on a wild goose chase. That is not acceptable."

2. "Marvin, that walkie-talkie on your belt is your immediate access to other employees that can help you with any issue that might arise. It is not acceptable for you not to use it and ask for help."

3. "Marvin, happy customers are repeat customers. Not doing whatever it takes within the scope of your job to make customers happy, is unacceptable."

4. "Marvin, when assisting customers, you can leave the produce section to assist them. To not assist a customer to your best ability is not acceptable. We recognize that this means that sometimes you will need to move with a customer to another part of the store for a short period of time. That is not only perfectly acceptable, it is what we want you to do."

5. "Marvin, if you are unclear if the customers wants you to take them personally to where an item is located, just ask them. Guess what? They will tell you if they can find their way as long as you point them in the right direct."

The rest of the story is clear cut. Once Marvin was informed that he was doing a poor job of assisting customers, what do you think happened?

Marvin was relieved. He could, and did, change the way he interacted with customers to include using the walkie-talkie and asking for help.

It was just that simple.

If any of Marvin's fellow experienced employees had just shown him the courtesy of their experience and how to interact with customers, it would not have taken four weeks for Marvin to understand that he needed to make a simple correction in his job performance in terms of assisting customers.

In this next case study, we will look at the flip side of the coin. Here we have a supervisor that not only tells his employees when they are performing poorly, he belittles them.

Case Study 4.4 Supervisor Superiority.

Scott was a first level supervisor working for a government agency with over 20 years of experience. The guy was reasonably smart, technically sound and knew his job very well. Although he complained a lot, he could always be counted on to meet his goals on or before schedule.

The only shortcoming Scott had, believe it or not, was Scott himself. For you see, Scott knew everything. Whether the subject was work related or related to what was the most reliable car to purchase, Scott knew it all and he had no problem telling anyone who would listen to him that very thing.

Scott was physically a large man and his whole persona was very intimidating. In fact, his "*know it all*" attitude earned him a nick name that everyone called him behind his back. He was known as "The Professor."

The Professor could belittle fellow employees and customers alike. The only reason he seemed to get away with it was because he again somehow always got his work done and made his goals. His past supervisors just seemed to gloss over his shortcomings.

Now Scott supervised two other employees and worked in partnership with several outside organizations as an integral part of his job. And beyond a shadow of a doubt the attitude he displayed worked against him. His employees did not like to be under his supervision. And the partner groups liked to stay clear of him if at all possible. His "*know it all*" demeanor was a negative to say the least. Nobody could do anything right but him and he let you know it.

In fact, his attitude was so bad that it became a limiting factor that kept him from being considered for promotions and positions of greater authority and responsibility within the agency.

It also made it difficult for other organizations to partner with him because his reputation went far and wide. It just seemed like everyone knew of his poor reputation and his "know it all" belittling attitude except Scott himself.

That is until he got a new supervisor. His new supervisor set him down and explained to him that he was doing a poor job in terms of his relationship skills with those he supervised, his customers, and the partners that worked hand in hand with his agency. The "know it all" belittling attitude had to stop.

The truly sad part about this case study is that we have all seen and worked with supervisors like Scott. Those that know everything and as a direct result exhibit poor relationship skills with employees they directly supervise, their peers, and perhaps most important of all, the customers.

And as remarkable or as unbelievable as it all sounds, Scott did not realize his shortcomings in terms of working with others. After all, his unit always made their goals.

No one had ever had the guts, or taken their role as his supervisor serious enough to be straightforward, honest, and direct with him. Not a single supervisor over his twenty years of employment with the agency.

So it probably won't surprise you to learn that when confronted with his "*attitude assessment*" by his new supervisor, Scott was shocked.

If fact, being told that he was belittling employees, customers and business partners was something he did not want to believe at first.

But he was fortunate enough to have a highly successful new supervisor that understood the importance of employee expectations.

This supervisor understood that all employees, even a know-it-all supervisor of others like Scott, expect to be told when they are doing a poor job, so that they can make the needed corrections.

You see Scott wanted to do well. Evidence of that is clear in the fact that he always could be counted on the meet or exceed his goals.

One of the negatives however of Scott's employment was that Scott didn't seem to care who he had to step on in order to make those goals. It was like his way of proving to the world that the unit he supervised was one of the best.

After Scott got over the initial shock of how he was doing a poor job in terms of his working relationships with others, he and his new supervisor began to work together to help him correct the deficiency.

I can tell you this much. It was not easy. Every once in a while, his supervisor would have to revisit the issue with Scott. And to be truthful, it took quite awhile for Scott to repair his reputation with customers and business partners.

But he did make the necessary changes and his peers eventually stopped calling him "The Professor." Many of his peers never thought they would see the day that Scott didn't give the appearance that he knew more than they did, but it did happen. And the organization was better for it, and so was Scott.

All of these improvements because Scott was blessed to have a new supervisor that was willing to assist him meet all of his employee expectations, even if Scott did not realize how important those were at the time.

Summary:

"To Know When They Are Doing a Poor Job."

From my experience, many supervisors fail miserably at this expectation. Telling an employee that they are doing a poor job may be scary and uncomfortable but it is the best option for both the employee and the supervisor. Again and let me repeat:

The overwhelming numbers of employees "want" to do a good job.

118

The overwhelming numbers of employees "<u>need</u>" to be able to do a good job.

The overwhelming numbers of employees "<u>expect</u>" that they can do a good job.

Giving feedback to an employee when that employee is doing a poor job should be viewed in the framework of giving that same employee an opportunity to do better and to improve.

In the overwhelming majority of cases, employees just need to have it made clear of what needs improvement and they will then work to make the needed corrections. It really is just all there is to it.

It should also be stated that the best time to point out areas of concern to an employee is when the deficiency first comes to light.

There is not a valid reason to delay such a discussion. Waiting to the end of some formal evaluation period to discuss poor performance is not meeting the expectations of that employee.

"Nip poor job performance in the bud before the situation gets out of hand."

For those supervisors that worry about how to correct employees when they are doing a poor job, let me assure of one thing. Just do it and take comfort that:

"It gets easier with time and experience."

119

EMPLOYEE EXPECTATIONS

The more experience you have working with employees and making the necessary course corrections, the easier it all becomes.

The reason for all of this is simple and straightforward. You are trying to help them become and stay successful. That is your reason for working to meet this expectation each and every day you supervise others.

Chapter 5- Fifth Expectation

"To Have the Training Needed."

Of the six employee expectations associated with employee success, this is the area that gives me the most pause.

I believe in the investment of resources to provide training.

I believe in the value of providing applicable and appropriate work related training.

And I believe that all employees, both inexperienced and seasoned veterans, appreciate the opportunity to receive the training they each need in order to be successful at their jobs.

There is this saying that goes something like this:

"*Everyone talks about the weather, but nobody ever does anything about it.*"

Well, I am here to tell you that:

"Everyone talks about training but nobody ever does anything about it."

How can any employee expect to be successful if they haven't been given the required training?

It is just asking for trouble in terms of loss of product, loss of time, lost efficiency and loss of customer service just to mention a few points concerning the negative effects of not providing the appropriate training needed to employees.

Most organizations have good intentions in terms of providing training to employees. But good intentions are not the same thing as following through with all of the different aspects of training.

From my experience and during those times of budget crisis, one of the first items cut nearly by all organizations in order to save money is the training program.

To put this whole concept of training in some type of perspective, let's consider the following list as the criteria needed for a good training program:

1. **Identify the training needed**
2. **Plan and organized the training.**
3. **Set aside the resources to carry out the training.**
4. **Conduct the training.**
5. **Evaluate the training completed**
6. **Follow up.**
7. **Refresher training as needed.**

There certainly can be discussion concerning these seven (7) listed aspects of a good training program to include consolidation into just five criteria, but that is not the point. So feel free to add or subtract to this list as you deem appropriate.

What is important, and is the essential point to be made here, is that in order to have a successful employee training program, the employer must make a considerable investment of time and other resources in order to carry out that program

It is also important to note that the training effort never ends and is ongoing throughout the working life of each and every employee in the organization.

Every person reading this book has worked at a job or in a work environment where you were not given the training you needed to carry out an assignment or a specific job.

We all have; but that does not make it right. It is the responsibility of the supervisor, in concert with each employee, to ensure that all employees under their care receive the training they need in order to be successful at their respective jobs or assignments.

I realize that me advising you of this is one thing. Actually providing training is something else.

How each supervisor goes about ensuring that the required training is carried out can be a daunting task from time to time; but that responsibility still rests with you and those employees under your charge to carry out.

Ultimately, the responsibility of receiving the correct and timely training should be given directly to each and every employee but the employee will need some guidance on what training to request.

Let's take a look at a case study that is one of my favorite stories that focuses on training, or lack thereof:

Case Study 5.1 Base Security

John Thomas was drafted into the U.S. Army at the tail end of the Vietnam War. After completing basic training at Ft. Leonard Wood in Missouri, followed by completion of combat medic training at Ft. Sam Houston in Texas, he was assigned his permanent duty station in West Germany.

Once he reached West Germany, John was then assigned to the 42nd Ambulance Company located at William O'Darby Kaserne in Furth, West Germany.

Three weeks after his arrival as a trained medic, John was reassigned to the Special Police division responsible for Gate Security for entrance and exit of all vehicles and personal, both civilian and military using the base. He was no longer a medic but was a part of base security and something he had absolutely no training in doing.

William O'Darby Kaserne was a major U.S. Army military installation housing combat ready artery and tank units as well as one military police unit and the 42nd Ambulance Company. Housed at the kaserne were many tanks, ambulances and artillery pieces essential to the mission of those respective units.

Entrance and exit to the kaserne could be accomplished by one of three base entrances: the east entrance, the north entrance and the main entrance on the west.

It should also be pointed out that William O'Darby Kaserne was set inside the city of Furth with civilian houses and business immediately adjacent to the U.S. military installation in this urban setting. Access to the military base was thus rather unimpeded for the most part by both civilian and military personnel at will.

John's tour of duty as a newly appointed member of the base Security Police was during the evening and overnight hours guarding one of the three entrances to the base on a rotating basis.

Training on what his responsibilities were as a Special Police Officer assigned to guard one of the entrances to the kaserne was non-existent. He didn't receive any.

It was as if he should just know what to do. He was simply told that whatever he did, he should not be caught sleeping in the guard shack in the morning when the brass started returning to the base. End of training.

Each night John Thomas was simply dropped off at one of the entrances at 1800 hours and remained there until 0700 the next day. There was a small guard shack at each entrance with a telephone that was connected to the other two guard shacks located inside. Each entrance was only staffed with a single guard for each shift. John would stand guard alone each night for 13 hours at one of the base entrances.

John soon discovered that the entire situation was bizarre, and in his own words, *"It was nothing but bulls—t."*

Base security was terribly lax and his follow Security Police comrades did not take their jobs very serious with the exception of making sure that they didn't look asleep in the morning.

People just came and went as they pleased at all hours of the night and the guards paid little attention to what was going on. Even German taxis came in and out of the base unimpeded. And on Sunday nights, when the mess halls were closed, pizza delivery vehicles frequented the base delivering pizza to the different units with the biggest violator being the military police unit itself.

After a couple of weeks of this nonsense, John asked Sergeant Hessup in charge of his shift if he could guard the main entrance to the base that night. He was given the assignment but with the stern warning that he had better not be sleeping when the General came through that entrance the next morning. It would be his first tour of duty guarding the main gate.

John then asked Hessup if there were any specific directions or duties he should know about.

The sergeant replied that in theory John should stop every civilian vehicle trying to enter the base and if that vehicle did not have the required base sticker mounted on the front bumper, then he should make the vehicle turn around and leave the base.

In addition, he should check to ensure that all people dressed in civilian clothes trying to enter the base on foot had the required base

126

IDs, or he was to deny those individuals entrance and send them back off base.

And lastly, when a vehicle entered the base and John recognized that the driver was an officer, he should salute the vehicle as it passed by. In addition, when the General's staff car came in, he should make a point of saluting that car as well.

But the kicker was the last piece of training advice that Sergeant Hessup gave John that night, *"Nobody ever does these things. All you need to do is to make sure that you are awake when the brass come through in the morning. That's all there is to it."*

This was the first real instruction that John had ever received in terms of what his duties were as a Special Police officer at William O'Darby Kaserne. But that instruction (training) was confusing:

"This is what you are supposed to do, but nobody ever does it that way."

So what did John do that night?

It was the perfect storm. Here John was half way around the world, drafted and taken away from his normal life all because he was born on the wrong day, stuck doing what amount to a useless job providing base security in a fashion that was obviously not taken seriously and was nothing but a joke.

EMPLOYEE EXPECTATIONS

John decided to change things up and follow the instructions that the sergeant gave him that night to the letter. He had no way of knowing if the training was legit or not, but he didn't care. He had been trained as a medic, and then randomly assigned to base security. If that is what the army wanted him to do and that made sense to somebody somewhere, then he would be the best damn Security Policeman he could be.

What real difference did it make anyway? He was only putting in his time until he was released from his military obligation. He was no career military man.

At around 0600 the next morning, people and cars tried to enter Darby through the main gate now guarded solely by John in the manner they usually entered that same gate each and every day.

But this morning would be different. John was standing in the middle of the road, away from the guard shack, directing traffic and checking IDs and vehicle stickers of all those trying to enter the base.

If someone tried to enter by foot and not in uniform or without the proper identification, John sent them packing.

Those trying to drive their private vehicles onto base that morning without the proper stickers prominently displayed, John had those same vehicles turn around and leave the base.

When a private vehicle with the proper sticker entered the base and John noticed the driver was an officer, he saluted the driver. And when the General's staff car came through the gate, he saluted the staff car as he let it pass as well.

John did this all according to Army regulations as he understood them but he had no way of knowing if he was correct or not. He was not a trained base security guard. All he had to go on was the short briefing Sergeant Hessup had given him just a few hours earlier.

Now since this was not really the usual procedure used to screen access onto the base each day, it made people mad as heck because the process slowed entrance onto the base to a crawl.

Some people actually ended up reporting to formation late as a direct result of John's decision and subsequent actions. And to top it all off, traffic was backed up for a couple of blocks around the corner onto the city streets of Furth just outside the base in this largely urban setting.

These same vehicles were now required to unexpectedly wait their turn in line to enter the base, while John checked IDs and stickers. Even the General's staff car had been stuck for a while in traffic as his driver made his way to the gate entrance where John stood as big as day alone in the middle of the street and in full control of the gate entrance.

EMPLOYEE EXPECTATIONS

It was no exaggeration that those trying to enter the base were hot and pissed off at the young SP standing guard on that particular morning. And those who were pissed off included officers, enlisted men and civilians all trying to enter Darby on that fateful morning.

Did John know he was making quite a stir? Yes he did, but what the heck could they do to him? He was following the brief guidance of Sergeant Hessup. And what were they going to do to him anyway, draft him again? Maybe take his rank of PFC away from him? John could have cared less. This was fun. It was the perfect storm.

At about 0715, Sergeant Hessup and the overall man in charge of the Security Police, Staff Sergeant Baker, both showed up in their jeep and started helping John sift through the foot and vehicle traffic still trying to enter the base.

Having three security guards helped to greatly speed up the process, and at about 0745 hours that morning the traffic slowed down to almost nothing again. Soon the traffic jam was over and John was sure that many folks who had tried to enter the base that morning did indeed not make their required 0700 formations.

John had made his point to the General and the top command staff about the lax base security. It was the most fun he had experienced since the day he was drafted.

As John was waving the last civilian vehicle through the gate and saluting the officer behind the wheel, Staff Sergeant Baker walked over to him. *"Well, Thomas. I want you to know that the General called my commanding officer first thing this morning. And then my commanding officer called me into his office. You know what the General wanted to talk about?"* Baker asked.

"The General wants to make you an officer," John replied in jest. It was all just too much fun.

"Not quite, but the General was damn impressed with the lone security guard on the main gate," Baker explained. *"He went on to say that it was the first time in nearly three years of being posted to this base that he had a base security guard that knew what the hell he was doing. And he didn't give a damn if it was an inconvenience for the troops or the civilian people working on Darby. He wants that type of security at every entrance gate each and every day from now on."*

John just looked at Baker and Hessup and smiled. *"Look, Sarg. I just did what you told me to do."*

"Well the General liked your efforts. He particularly liked your smart salute. And he liked the way your uniform looked. Man Thomas, you made me look damn good. Would you like a full time job in base security? I could use a guy like you," Baker continued.

EMPLOYEE EXPECTATIONS

"Thanks for the offer, but I don't know anything about security. I am a medic. And I want to stay a medic and when my SP tour is over, I am not staying."

As I said, this is one of my favorite case studies to tell others. In a way there is humor to whole perfect storm thing and for John Thomas and the two sergeants it all worked out well for them.

For a 19 year old kid, John had taken a calculated risk. A risk that for all he knew could have backfired in his face big time. The advantage he had was this. He did not care if he got fired. He had not asked to be drafted into the army in the first place; but that is not really the point. This is the point.

"When employees are not given the training they need to do their jobs, they will improvise."

Untrained employees will guess how they should do their job. What alternative do they have? And if you have an employee like a John Thomas that wants to make a very public point about lack of training, the end results can be far more than just embarrassing, they can be disastrous.

I have seen untrained employees make decisions and take actions that are incorrect and cost the company money. Whether it is making the wrong parts, using the wrong materials or working on low priority projects, it is a fact that untrained employees can be a liability to themselves and the organization.

Trust me, I do get it.

132

John Thomas got away with a risky approach to making his point, but I know this man. If he had seriously and respectfully been given the needed training on how to do the job of guarding the gate as a member of base security, he would have followed those instructions to the letter.

After all, the base was full of combat ready equipment that was deemed essential to the protection of West Germany and our other European allies. Not much gets more important than that.

One of the most common reasons that employees make mistakes, costly or otherwise, is simply because they have not received the required training to do their jobs. Period.

Your job as a supervisor is to remember that employees expect, and deserve, to be given the needed training to do their jobs.

Whether that training is in a formal setting or on-the-job training is not as important as simply receiving the training in whatever format.

It is your job as a supervisor to remind your employer that:

"Training is not a cost.

"Training is an investment."

Just be sure to keep the training appropriate, applicable and timely.

The next case study illustrates how the lack of training can be costly to the organization.

133

Case Study 5.2 Bad Parts.

Marie worked as a factory worker in the Truckmeyer FT Gauge Co. After working at her current job for two years, Marie applied for a new position in the small gauge assembly department and was looking forward to her new job.

The job paid more per hour and she could earn an extra hourly incentive payment which added to her weekly income.

Her new position was a "timed" position and she needed to assemble a certain number of small high pressure water gauges each hour. As part of that job she needed to cut pieces of copper tubing to length and then flatten these pieces out and form then into a semicircle for insertion into the body of the gauge.

Marie was proficient at cutting the pieces and the rest of the work needed to assemble the gauges she was responsible for. The only catch was that when her gauges were tested for accuracy, nearly 50% of them did not pass tolerance levels and were subsequently rejected.

Not only was Marie not making any incentive at her new position, she was costing the company money.

When the quality control people realized that Marie was apparently struggling with her job, they informed Marie's supervisor and then a

team went to investigate and determine what Marie was doing wrong.

What they found was that Marie was missing one important step in the process of cutting the copper tubing to length. She was not sharpening the saw blade used in the process periodically to ensure a clean and smooth cut.

All of Marie's cut pieces of tubing had ragged ends that were not smooth allowing for a less than tight fit which was throwing the tolerance levels of her finished gauges out of whack.

The reason for all of this was simple. Marie had never been trained on the importance of keeping the saw blade sharp or just how to sharpen the blade.

For those of us that have worked in a factory making widgets, we have all experienced something similar to this case study that took place right before our very eyes. In fact, it might have happened directly to you.

Something similar has happened to me as an employee on more than one occasion where I was not given all of the training I needed in order to be successful in various work related situations.

In Marie's case the fix was simple. Once she learned how to keep the saw blade sharp, her assembled gauges were quality gauges that rarely failed tolerance tests.

The really unfortunate aspect of the case study, and one that is rather common, is that the other employees working with Marie had enough experience to know that she would have problems if she didn't keep the metal saw blade sharp. Everyone knew. What idiot wouldn't know that?

In this case, her peers just kept quiet and went about their business knowing that at some point Marie was going to fail and they would all get a good laugh.

I know it all sounds so simple, and it is really. Marie expected to receive the required training she needed in order to do her new job, and for whatever reason, purposeful or not, she was not given that training. In fact, important helpful information was deliberately being withheld from her by her peers just for the sake of screwing with the new person.

I suppose it is the indoctrination principle, or hazing principle run amuck.

"Let's make fun of the new person because they could not possibly have the experience to do this job. The new person needs to learn the job the hard way, just like I did when I started. It will be fun to see them struggle."

The unfortunate part is that Marie's supervisor should have made sure that she was fully trained in all aspects of her new job before these unnecessary course corrections had to be made.

What he failed to do was to assign her a competent trainer to teach her all of the aspects of gauge assembly. And he also should have known how the employees under his care would treat the new "kid on the block."

Here is another important aspect of training:

"Not all employees make good trainers!"

136

In Marie's case, the trainer that had been assigned to her by her supervisor was an employee named Darrell. Darrell was competent at gauge assembly and was one of the top performers in the department, but he was a terrible trainer and did not relate well with others.

So even though Darrell did not purposefully mislead or steer Marie in the wrong direction, he simply left out one important piece of training that was a vital cog for employee success; sharpening the saw blade.

Darrell was not well organized and training other people was something he just felt uncomfortable doing and his peers in the department knew he was a poor trainer.

As a supervisor, it is likely that you will not be directly involved in providing all the training that each of the employees under your care need, deserve and expect to receive. But you can have a direct and important impact to ensure that those who are providing the training are capable of being competent trainers.

Choose wisely.

You need to select trainers that are not only competent in the different technical aspects of the job, but enjoy the duties associated with training others.

You need to select trainers that work well with others and have good communication skills.

You need to select trainers that care about the success of the company and the success of those they train. In short, you want a trainer that will take ownership in providing training to others.

EMPLOYEE EXPECTATIONS

In the next case study, let's look at the expectation of having the required training in order to do the job from a totally different perspective that is often times overlooked.

Case Study 5.3 Medical Emergency.

Ted, Paul, and George made up a three man survey crew for the Johnstony, Johnstony and Evans Construction Firm specializing in the construction of farm ponds.

One hot July afternoon, the trio was surveying a site for a new farm pond that was several miles away from the nearest farmstead and even further from the nearest town.

As the survey progressed, Paul was running the transit while Ted and George were some distance away running the survey rod and setting wooded survey stakes into the ground.

All of the sudden and without warning, Paul collapsed to ground and was not moving. Both Ted and George had seen Paul fall and immediately stopped what they were doing and rushed to assist Paul.

When they reached Paul, they found him unconscious but still breathing. Ted immediately started to administer first aide while George got on the radio and called for an ambulance to come to the site.

Later that afternoon, Paul was in a recovery room at a local hospital where a pacemaker

138

had been installed to correct the irregular heart beat that was the apparent reason for his collapse.

In this case study, the Johnstony, Johnstony and Evans Construction Firm had provided all of their employees with first-aid and CPR training before allowing them to operate in remote and isolated areas where there would not be immediate access to medical personnel.

This construction firm understood the importance of protecting their employees and to provide them with the safest working environment as possible. And even though the possibly of having a medical emergency on a survey site was not likely, it could happen. Johnstony, Johnstony and Evans wanted all of their employees trained to handle such emergencies.

We will address safety more in the next chapter but the issue needs to be addressed here as well as a training expectation.

As a supervisor, employees under your care expect that you will ensure that they are provided the necessary training to be safe and to react to any medical emergency that may come their way.

Such training could include, but certainly not limited to: the location of first-aid and other emergency equipment and supplies, how to contact emergency medical personnel in house or otherwise, and how to act in case of medical or natural disaster emergencies.

EMPLOYEE EXPECTATIONS

Summary:

"To Have the Training Needed."

Again I want to reemphasize that of the six employee expectations associated with employee success, this is the area that gives me the most pause. All organizations have good intentions to provide the best and timely training they can for employees so that all employees have the knowledge, skills and abilities to do their jobs.

But in the hustle and bustle of doing the business of the company, training often times gets overlooked, set aside or provided in a less than quality fashion.

I get that.

I have seen this happen in every single company, agency or organization that I have worked for over the years. But that does not make it right, nor is it what employees expect from their employers.

"Everyone talks about training but nobody ever does anything about it."

The case studies provided in the chapter are not meant to be all encompassing in terms of the issues associated with not providing the necessary training for employees do their respective jobs.

These case studies are only provided to stimulate your thinking to help you identify short comings you, or your organization, have in terms of meeting the important employee expectation of having the required training to do their jobs.

140

It is up to each supervisor to fully embrace this employee expectation and work each day to ensure that employee training takes place as applicable and appropriate for each and every employee under their direction and care.

Chapter 6- Sixth Expectation

"To Work Under Safe Conditions and Have the Necessary Equipment and Resources."

This expectation should also be self explanatory and straightforward, and yet this expectation is routinely not being met in businesses across this country each and every day.

Ladies and gentleman, no business should allow their employees to work in an unsafe environment at any time, period.

The good news is that supervisors have some control over this expectation and can make a huge difference in ensuring safety on the job.

Likewise, no business should require their employees to operate without the necessary equipment and resources in order to efficiently and effectively do their job.

The good news here is also that supervisors can have some control over ensuring that the necessary equipment and resources are available for employees to do their job.

"To Work Under Safe Conditions"

In the workplace all employees expect to work in a safe environment. No employee wants to be hurt either physically or emotionally on the job.

In today's workplace, safety has become a working theme or motto in many organizations. In fact, if you go on line and complete an online job application for one of those big box stores, you will find questions about an applicant's understanding and willingness to follow all safety rules and procedures dominate the questions being asked.

Here is one of my favorites from those applications that goes something like this:

"Safety policy requires you not to do something, but you have figured out a way to accomplish your job quicker and at the same time save the company money. Your method would require you to overlook one little aspect of the safety policy, even though you are convinced that in this one instance by overlooking the safety policy, nobody would be in danger.

Do you go ahead and do the job your way using your method and then explain how you saved the company money later?"

Answering "yes" to this question is a quick way for an applicant to not be considered for hiring. In fact the issue of safety and following policy is so ingrained in these online applications, that the question is asked multiple times and in multiple fashions throughout the job application just to ensure that your answers are consistent in terms of respecting company established safety policies.

And I get that.

Employers don't want to see employees get hurt on the job, period. And their human resource and legal departments want to deal with injured employees even less. Trying to gauge a job applicant's commitment to

143

following company safety policies is simply standard practice in the business world of today.

In this next case study, we will examine an approach that one company uses to ensure their employees operate in a safe environment.

Case Study 6.1 Pesticide Spray.

FarmZT Tech employed many field employees that provided on farm assistance to their agricultural clients.

Services provided by the company included on site soil sampling; pest scouting and monitoring, and field by field fertilizer and soil fertility recommendations.

In order to do this, FarmZT Tech employees were commonly working onsite in many different farm fields to provide service to their clientele.

As an employer, FarmZT Tech was required by federal and state law(s) to provide a workplace free of known health and safety hazards to all of their employees.

And since the standard practice used by most of their farm clientele to spray crop production fields for both weed and insect pests was very common, the FarmZT Tech leadership made a decision to change company policy in terms of

144

how field employees conducted their business.

In a concerted effort to protect their employees from potential unsafe working conditions, company policies were changed to reflect when employees would be allowed to work in farm fields that were sprayed with pesticides.

Under no conditions were employees required or even allowed onto any farm field that was recently sprayed with a pesticide. Entrance on such fields would be delayed until time it was deemed safe in concert with the labeling instructions provided by the chemical manufacturer.

This case study reflects a significant cultural change in how business was conducted at FarmZT Tech. Until the passage of the federal "right-to-know" laws, many employers did not think too much about the safety of their employees in terms of chemicals in the workplace.

While it was certainly true that FarmZT Tech employees were never actually in a farm field at the same time fields were being sprayed, that did not mean there wasn't still some pesticide residue remaining in the field afterwards.

FarmZT Tech established minimum wait times before employees were allowed on the fields and provided protective equipment and clothing as recommended by state and federal safety guidelines.

Considerable effort has been made in recent years to ensure employee safety in the workplace relative to exposure to different health hazards to include workplace chemicals. Companies like FarmZT Tech have been leaders in working to provide a safe workplace for all of their employees.

It is perhaps easy to understand that working around agricultural chemicals should require special efforts to protect employees. We all get that. But it should be pointed out that it is very common in most work environments to be subject to exposure to some type of chemical listed in the federal "right-to-know laws that should be addressed. This is true even in an office work environment.

In this case study, we will discuss the very real dangers of not following proven safety standards in the workplace.

Case Study 6.2 Trench Collapse.

Bill Jones worked as an engineering technician to provide onsite engineering inspection for the engineering company that he work for in the eastern part of the state.

One late fall afternoon, Bill was on a job site providing the inspection services for drainage tile being installed adjacent to a building site. The tile installation was being done by a private contractor and Bill was there to oversee the installation to ensure that the installation met the standards of the contract.

At one point in the installation, the contractor was cutting through a small hill and trying to keep a down sloping grade for the tile that was

being installed. The earthen trench the contractor had carved out in the hill was now running between nine (9) and ten (10) feet in depth and the soil had become sandy.

Concerned about the sand pocket and what he needed to do to address the sand, the contractor crawled down into the trench.

Not only did the contractor crawl into the trench, Bill Jones followed suit and jumped into the trench as well. Neither Bill Jones nor the contractor were wearing hardhats, but that did not stop either man. Wearing the required hardhats was just something they didn't do very often.

The two men were only in the trench for just a couple of minutes when the trench collapsed and both men were buried in a manner of seconds.

The contractor was killed. Bill Jones survived but lost his right ear in the trench collapse.

Sometimes, as a supervisor, you have to be the "hard guy" in terms of requiring that all employees operate in a safe manner while carrying out the terms of their employment.

I say this because I have seen employees decide on their own, and for whatever the reason, to not wear the protective wear. And it doesn't matter who the employer is, if the supervisor allows employees to skip wearing protective clothing, employees will violate policy and "risk" it.

Whether we talk about a hardhat, a protective vest, or protective gloves, it doesn't matter. And it doesn't matter that the task at hand that requires protective wear is only short term. The gear must be worn each and every time, period.

This accident could have been avoided if Bill Jones had followed company policy in terms of working around trenches and wearing the correct protective wear.

Specifically, Bill Jones should never have jumped down into that trench. And he should never have allowed the contractor to do so either. Bill Jones had the power, as the onsite inspector, to shut down the operation if the contractor was not operating in a safe manner, but he chose not to do that.

It is a fact that both Bill Jones and the contractor were both experienced professionals and they certainly knew they were not following the prescribed safety rules.

Both also understood that an earthen trench, that exceeded a certain maximum depth, required that each side be shorn up with bracing to prevent collapse before anyone was allowed to climb down into that trench.

This action was an Occupational Health and Safety Administration (OHSA) requirement; and that requirement was undisputable and was put into place to prevent such tragedies from occurring.

It is very likely that if the contractor had followed OHSA regulations and installed the required trench bracing before he entered the trench, the accident would most likely not have occurred

It was later determined by medical staff that Bill would not have likely lost an ear if he had been wearing a hardhat. There was also speculation that the contractor would have survived the trench collapse if he too had been wearing a hardhat.

Safety is something that must be embedded in the normal routine of all employees. In most big box stores there is usually a sign posted in the break room or elsewhere that keeps track of the consecutive days without an accident.

Milestones related directly to such safety records are often times celebrated. That is just one method of trying to keep safety concerns as part of the normal day to day operation of a successful business.

Please be reminded that even though employees expect to work under safe conditions, there will be times that you will need to correct them from shirking safety considerations. YOU OWE THEM THAT!

Let me finish with an example that is seldom discussed but does exist in the workplace.

Case Study 6.3 Sexual Harassment.

One calm Friday morning, Tim Smothers received a phone call from his immediate supervisor, Sally Harker, the regional manager for the company that he worked for in panhandle of Texas.

The call was short and to the point and went something like this:

"I just received a call from one of your interns in one your offices. It seems that she is being sexually harassed by a

customer and her supervisor has done nothing to stop it. I don't know what to tell you, but you need to fix it. And I suggest you fix it now. Good luck. Oh, one last point. This customer is an elected official."

Tim Smothers was shocked. He knew the intern's supervisor very well and the last thing he expected was to hear that he did not address the issue of sexual harassment of one of his female employees.

The first action Tim took was to call the supervisor who was at home as he had taken the day off.

To Tim's shock, this supervisor admitted that he was aware of the sexual harassment complaint and had told his female intern that he would handle the situation when he had time. At the present, it was too busy with other things and would get to it as soon as possible.

No employee needs to be subject to sexual harassment. Few things can destroy an employee's workplace environment and sense of safety than to be the subject to sexual harassment.

In this case study, Tim Smothers dropped everything he was doing and traveled immediately to the office where the sexual harassment was alleged to have occurred.

He did this for three reasons: (1) To get a firsthand understanding of the issues involved; (2) To reassure the employee that sexual harassment would not be tolerated and that Tim would move heaven and earth to immediately halt the unwanted treatment by the customer. And to further ensure and make his point, he wanted her to know that he didn't need her immediate supervisor to make that happen. The ball was now in Tim's lap and he would handle it. And (3) To determine what needed to be done to correct the situation to the satisfaction of the female intern.

When Tim arrived onsite and interviewed the intern, he found the situation to be more involved than what he was led to believe.

Not only was the customer putting his hands on the intern, this same gentleman was harassing other female employees as well; and the immediate supervisor was indeed dragging his heals in terms of dealing with the situation.

Tim was an experienced and highly successful supervisor. And even though this particular situation was intense, and was somewhat convoluted, he was able to resolve the issues to the satisfaction of the females employees involved, and to do so immediately without any further delay.

The key to his success was to address the issues in a straightforward and no nonsense manner as the most urgent and highest priority assignment at that time. Everything else went on the back burner. Nothing was a higher priority.

Tim was determined to make the workplace again a safe environment for those female employees. That is what employees expect; and that is exactly what Tim did.

Of course the direct supervisor of the intern had a price to pay in terms of his inaction through subsequent training and interaction with Tim Smothers; but as we have already discussed, *"Employees expect to be told when they are doing a poor job."* Tim would meet that employee expectation and then some.

"To Have the Necessary Equipment and Resources"

In the workplace all employee expect to have the necessary equipment to do their job. How can any employee become successful if they don't have the resources to do their respective job?

It is my observation that in the construction industry, contractors have figured this one out. The rest of us have lessons yet to learn. It doesn't matter if we are talking about an electrical contractor, a plumbing contractor or a roofing contractor, they all have their specialized tools and equipment to make their jobs easier and more successful.

The same is true with mechanics. Their whole existence is based on having the correct tool to deal with the ever changing world of automotive repair and maintenance.

Supervisors that came up through the system as one of the worker bees often times have this expectation figured out. I commend them for that on-the-job working experience enables them to understand the importance of having the needed equipment and resources for employees to do their jobs.

They have been there, done that.

What is common about these same supervisors is this. They mistakenly think that if they meet this employee expectation, the other five expectations will be minor.

Idiots.

Well, maybe not idiots, but basing your entire supervisory role solely on ensuring that all employees have the best equipment is foolish.

The flip side of the coin is this. There are also those supervisors that overlook this expectation for the most part and think employees can "get by" with the equipment they already have.

Let's take a look at this next case study to reflect one aspect of employee expectation number six.

Case Study 6.4 Utility Knives.

Tracy was a new BigBox-BigDeal department store employee. Her job was simple and straightforward for the most part. She stocked the shelves in the grocery section of the store.

The position required her to open up large boxes of product so that she could restock the shelves with the contents inside each of these large product boxes.

As a tool to aid in this process, her supervisor gave her a used utility knife for use in cutting into the outside of the cardboard containers so that she could get at the contents.

This particular knife was well used and did not open very easily and in many ways was a safety hazard. In addition, the blade was dull and Tracy had no idea of how to replace the blade or even where the replacement blades were located.

EMPLOYEE EXPECTATIONS

After several weeks of struggling with the dull blade and the less that quality utility knife, one of her coworkers noticed the condition of her knife one day as he was working side by side with her in the grocery section.

When he asked her why she was using such a piece of crap, she told him that that was the utility knife she was given to do her job.

The coworker laughed and led Tracy to a metal locker and opened it up and reached inside to retrieve a brand new utility knife for Tracy to use. He then also showed her how to replace dull blades and where she could find replacement blades.

He also got her a pair of gloves she could wear when handling frozen items in the freezer section of the grocery department.

Just having the necessary and functional equipment made Tracy happy and enabled her to be more efficient in her job.

It always amazes me how ill-prepared supervisors are to supply new employees with the tools they need to do their job when the employees begin their new positions on that first day.

Remarkable, and in my mind, totally foolish and unproductive.

For any employee stocking shelves, some type of box cutter is essential in order to be able to do their job. That fact is not rocket science. That fact is just the reality of the "stocker" position.

154

I once worked for a grocery chain that was very employee oriented. As a stocker, we all carried box cutters as one of the tools used to do our jobs. And if we needed a new one, or needed new blades, a supply was always right at hand.

Now I understand that box cutters get misplaced and are accidentally taken home for whatever reason; and as such there is an expense to replacing box cutters frequently, but that issue is not insurmountable to resolve either.

Installing and utilizing small individual employee lockers used to house company aprons, vests, box cutters; etc is an easy solution to replacing these types of tools frequently. At the end of each shift, employees just return these items to their assigned individual lockers.

But even having a locker system can be inappropriately administered by management. I have seen large box stores with rows of the individual lockers stand empty.

A locker is not automatically assigned to new employees when they enter the workforce but are only assigned when new employees sometime later report to HR who is responsible for locker assignments. It sometimes takes weeks for a new employee to feel comfortable enough and then make a special effort to venture over to HR to get a locker.

In this next case study, we will discuss difference of opinions concerning the type of resources needed.

Case Study 6.5 "No" to GPS Units.

The SupraGP Ag Environmental Support (SAES) Company specialized in restoring wetlands on agricultural lands in the upper Midwest.

The company President, James Hillcrest, had seven (7) different regional managers under him that were responsible for SAES operations in their respective regions.

These seven different regions operated autonomously under the rules and direction of the main central office located in St. Paul, MN. Each regional manager was given an operating budget to include an equipment and supply budget to manage according to the needs of the region.

Debra Brown managed the far southeastern region and was a well respected and accomplished regional manager. She supervised a talented and innovative crop of professionals that were outstanding in their respective fields of wetland restoration on private lands.

As new technology advanced, Debra's team discovered that they could greatly decrease the amount of time spent in the field surveying and laying out wetlands if they just adopted Global Positioning System (GPS) technology in their operations.

In fact, it was determined that the team could save as much as 20-30 hours per wetland restoration if GPS technology was used as a tool in their business with the data points being directly downloaded into a company computer. This approach allowed the wetland boundary information to be transferred efficiently in digital format to digital aerial photography of the wetland site.

Debra was so excited about the possibilities of the adoption of such GPS units that she contacted President Hillcrest directly and informed him that she was going to use some of her equipment budget to begin the process of outfitting her region with GPS units to improve efficiency; and at the same time increase company profits in her region.

But the reaction she received from President Hillcrest surprised her. Hillcrest was lukewarm to the idea of using company funds for these foolish GPS units. His position was the she didn't need new toys to do her job. The company was able to delineate wetlands before GPS units were invented and he wasn't convinced the new technology was anything more than new technology.

But he would not go back on his word. He had given Debra an equipment budget to manage as she deemed fit, and he would not stop her. If she wanted to invest in GPS units, that was her business.

That is where the discussion ended, or at least that is what Debra had thought. Later when Debra ordered three (3) GPS from the vendors that SAES used, President Hillcrest called her directly and berated her judgment.

And to make matters worse, and to teach Debra a lesson, he cut her equipment and supply budget in half since she obviously did not know how to manage it. Even though Debra had consulted him first and got his reluctant approved to purchase GPS units in the first place, all of that did not matter. President Hillcrest was teaching Debra a lesson about mismanagement of company funds.

The rest of the story goes something like this. When the other regional managers heard that Debra had purchased GPS units, they too recognized the value that such technology had to the bottom line of their respective regions and went out and purchased a small number of the units for their respective regions as well.

The only difference was that they did not tell President Hillcrest about their plans. They just did it.

One year later, the adoption and use of GPS units as a mainstream tool of the company was seen as the biggest positive step the company had made to improve the company's bottom line in over 10 years.

In fact, President Hillcrest was so impressed with the results that in the next year's equipment budget, he included a line item to purchase GPS units across the board in all regions to complete the unfilled requests for the new technology.

Here is the deal about early and later adopters of new technology. It happens in every company and business. The trick is to learn which technology is worth the investment and which technology should be passed up.

President Hillcrest never did reconcile the beratement and punishment he inflicted on Debra for the positive decision she had made for the company. He never brought it up and she didn't either. After all, it wasn't about either one of them. It was about ensuring that the employees had the proper resources to do their job.

Having the resources to do their job is not only about having the right equipment and tools. It is also about having and utilizing the best procedures and processes to do the job.

In my experience, the best ideas to improve the day to day operations of the company come from the employees themselves. And if a new process, or way of doing business has been put forth and has validity, then employees expect to be able to use the new process, and justifiably so.

Just because something has always been done one way, doesn't make it the best and most efficient way to conduct business. Wise managers and supervisors encourage employee input and suggestions on how to improve the processes used in the organization.

President Hillcrest also had a bug up his butt about spending "extra" money on four wheel drive vehicles for his field employees. Again, his position was what did the company do before 4x4 vehicles? The company was built and survived just fine without 4x4 vehicles in the past and it didn't need such vehicles now.

I can also report to you that President Hillcrest eventually came around on the issue of 4x4 vehicles as well. It only took a couple of times of him providing direct supervision to the field and getting stuck adjacent to wetlands for him to see the value of upgrading his fleet of vehicles. Sounds silly now, but all businesses providing on farm assistance and services had to learn that lesson the hard way.

Summary:

"To Work Under Safe Conditions and Have the Necessary Equipment and Resources."

Without a question of a doubt, employees expect to do work in a safe environment and have the equipment and resources to do their job.

In this chapter I have outlined several case studies that only are a small tip of the iceberg in terms of situations regarding employee safety.

It is your job as the immediate supervisor to assess the safety conditions of your worksite and make any corrections that you need to make.

It is your job to ensure that any required safety training is identified, planned and conducted.

It is your job to require that 100% of the safety policies of your organization are followed by every single employee, even if you have to get tough and set your foot down. That is your job.

It is also your responsibility to look after each of your employees even when those same employees are their own worst enemy in terms of following safety rules and procedures. If you need to remind them to be safe,

160

then remind them to be safe.

And then when it comes to ensuring that each employee has the needed resources to do their jobs, your responsibility also never stops.

Whether supplying simple items such as a utility knife, or something more encompassing like a GPS unit, you want to ensure that each and every employee has the equipment to be successful in their respective jobs.

Ladies and gentleman, and as I have stated before, no business should allow their employees to work in an unsafe environment at any time, period.

Likewise, no business should require their employees to operate without the necessary equipment and resources in order to efficiency and effectively do their job.

Moving Forward

This handbook is a reference focusing on six employee expectations; the understanding of which is fundamental to the success of both new and experienced supervisors.

Those of us that supervise come to appreciate that supervision is an art form. It is an art form that must be molded with time and experience in an ever changing work environment.

Recognizing employee expectations of their supervisor, and then exercising good judgment in trying to meet those expectations, is the platform for success in working with and through others.

I of course do recognize that the employee expectation listing as outlined in this book is not all encompassing.

"I do realize that employees EXPECT TO GET PAID."

"I do realize that employees EXPECT TO HAVE EMPLOYEE BENEFITS."

My purpose of this book is not to outline the obvious, but to address the employee expectations that will take some effort and commitment to address on a daily basis.

It is my contention that each and every supervisor that understands, adopts, and works to meet the employee expectations outlined in the proceeding chapters will find their job more enjoyable and rewarding.

Let me finish with the last secret about employee expectations. These six employee expectations, plus adding getting paid and having benefits, can really be boiled down to just **one**.
That's correct.
The six employee expectations employees have of their supervisor can be boiled down to just one. The other five expectations are really just subparts of the main expectation as first listed in chapter 1:

"To Be Treated Equitably, Fairly and with Dignity and Respect."

If you ensure that employees under your care *know what their job is*...........it can be argued that you are <u>*treating them equitably, fairly, and with dignity and respect.*</u>

If you tell employees under your care *when they are doing a good job*...........it can be argued that you are <u>*treating them equitably, fairly, and with dignity and respect*</u>.

If you tell employees under your care *when they are doing a poor job*............it can be argued that you are <u>*treating them equitably, fairly, and with dignity and respect*</u>.

EMPLOYEE EXPECTATIONS

If you ensure that employees under your care *have the training needed*...........it can be argued that you are *treating them equitably, fairly, and with dignity and respect.*

If you ensure that employees under your care *work under safe conditions and have the necessary equipment and resources*.......it can be argued that you are *treating them equitably, fairly, and with dignity and respect.*

In my efforts to provide training to supervisors on meeting employee expectations, I have made it my purpose to define these expectations in terms of these six interconnected expectations in some detail.

It has been my experience that to fully understand the impact of treating employee equitably, fairly and with dignity and respect, a more complete discussion and dialog must take place that includes the totality of what has been outlined for you in the preparation of this handbook.

The key now is for you to embrace the concepts outlined and work to make them an integral part of your normal day to day operation as a supervisor.

If you do that, and as you continue in your supervisor role, you will find more joy providing direction to those under your care.

My suggestion is that you keep this handbook close by as a reference, and begin by making a self assessment of where you are at the present in terms of meeting employee expectations (See Appendix A) to use as a starting point, a baseline.

Once you have identified the areas where you need to improve, develop an individual training plan for yourself, complete with actions you plan to take to improve and a time frame in which to complete those actions specific to you and your workplace, and then follow that plan.

This action plan can be as detailed as you deem appropriate but it should be written down as a self improvement agreement you make with yourself.

And then periodically do a self evaluation of your progress in how well you have adopted and are putting to use the principles outlined in the handbook (See Appendix B) as it relates directly, but not limited to the action plan you developed for yourself above.

It is my experience, and belief, that you will see a marked improvement in your score, but more importantly you will see a marked improvement in your daily interactions with your reports.

It has been my honor to share these thoughts with you. I have the most admiration for those of you that are, or will be, highly successful supervisors.

The role of supervisor is both challenging and rewarding in ways that are in a continual state of change. But it is all worthwhile in the end.

The American spirit in the workforce is based on the interactions of people just like you.

Congratulations.

And best wishes.

EMPLOYEE EXPECTATIONS

I leave you will a brief listing of the "do's" and "don't" of maintaining good relationships with employees under your direction and care that I share with all of those that I train:

"**Do**" eat soup with a spoon.
"**Don't**" eat soup with a fork.

"**Do**" praise employees for work well done."
"**Don't**" criticize employees in front of others."

"**Do**" embrace the six employee expectations.
"**Don't**" overlook the six employee expectations.

"**Do**" respect employee input."
"**Don't**" insult the dignity of an employee."

"**Do**" be firm but humble and respectful."
"**Don't**" be arrogant and uppity."

"**Do**" respect your employees as valuable assets."
"**Don't**" think of your employees as subordinates."

Appendix A. Baseline Evaluation

Complete a self evaluation by checking the appropriate blank consisted with your current level of achievement.

	*1**	*2**	*3**	*4**	*5**
To Be Treated Equitably, Fairly and with Dignity and Respect.	—	—	—	—	—
To Know What Their Job Is.	—	—	—	—	—
To Know When They Are Doing a Good Job.	—	—	—	—	—
To Know When They Are Doing a Poor Job.	—	—	—	—	—
To Have the Training Needed.	—	—	—	—	—
To Work Under Safe Conditions and Have the Necessary Equip. and Resources.	—	—	—	—	—

* 1 is the lowest score, 5 is the highest score.

Appendix B. Periodic Progress Evaluations

Complete a self evaluation by checking the appropriate blank consisted with your current level of achievement.

	1*	*2**	*3**	*4**	*5**
To Be Treated Equitably, Fairly and with Dignity and Respect.	—	—	—	—	—
To Know What Their Job Is.	—	—	—	—	—
To Know When They Are Doing a Good Job.	—	—	—	—	—
To Know When They Are Doing a Poor Job.	—	—	—	—	—
To Have the Training Needed.	—	—	—	—	—
To Work Under Safe Conditions and Have the Necessary Equip. and Resources.	—	—	—	—	—

* 1 is the lowest score, 5 is the highest score.

About the Author

John T. Nicholson has decades of first-hand experience working in manufacturing, retail, and both the civilian and defense sides of the federal government. He has provided training to countless supervisors on the various aspects of supervision and management.

His professional career has taken him to ten different states that include: Arkansas, Iowa, Kansas, Missouri, Minnesota, Nebraska, New York, Oklahoma, South Carolina and Texas. In addition, he has worked and provided management support internationally in Guam and Germany.

*Contact John at employeeexpectations@gmail.com with comments or inquiries

Other Titles

The Joy of "Supervising Downhill"
Nicholson & Nicholson Publishing (2013)
**www.Amazon.com
**www.barnesandnoble.com

In this book, Nicholson provides a unique approach to outline his principles, guidelines and rules for successful supervision. His practical approach is predicated on real life supervisory experience molded into an understandable must read for those directly involved in the role of supervisor.

Seven (7) guiding principles are discussed and outlined using a simple acronym (B-I-C-Y-C-L-E) that will aid in remembrance of these fundamental principles

> B - **Bring a positive "can do" attitude.**
> I - **Infuse an atmosphere of respect for each and every employee.**
> C - **Communicate with integrity in an open and transparent fashion.**
> Y - **Yearn to be the best supervisor you can be.**
> C - **Consort with other highly successful supervisors.**
> L - **Lead by positive example.**
> E - **Earn respect as a supervisor each and every day.**

Both newly selected and experienced supervisors will benefit greatly from using the simple principles outlined in this book. Nicholson outlines and converts the mistakes and successes from his personal supervisory experience into a remarkable hands-on supervisory guide.

www.ingramcontent.com/pod-product-compliance
Lightning Source LLC
Chambersburg PA
CBHW070241190526
45169CB00001B/254